THE DAWN OF HOPE

AN ADVENT DEVOTIONAL
BASED ON LUKE 2

JOE HENSON

Scripture quotations are taken from the Authorized (King James) Version unless otherwise stated. Rights in the Authorized Version in the United Kingdom are vested in the Crown. Reproduced by permission of the Crown's patentee, Cambridge University Press.

Scripture quotations marked (ERV) taken from the Holy Bible: Easy-to-Read Version (ERV), International Edition © 2013, 2016 by Bible League International and used by permission.

ISBN: 979-8-89316-476-3 - eBook
ISBN: 979-8-89316-477-0 - Paperback

To Garthea, my beloved wife and partner in life's journey; to Joseph and Garth, our sons who've grown into loving husbands and devoted fathers, and their wives, Kristi and Becky—your commitment to leading your families in godliness fills us with gratitude; and to our eight precious grandchildren, who bring boundless joy to our lives.

This book is a testament to the legacy of love, faith, and hope that flows through our family.

Your presence in my life has been a constant source of inspiration, bringing to mind a thousand cherished memories that have shaped this work.

As each new dawn heralds fresh hope, so, too, does each generation of our family carry forward the light of love and faith.

This work is dedicated to you all, my beacons of hope and harbingers of a brighter tomorrow.

May the words herein reflect the depth of gratitude I feel to God for the blessing of our family and the journey we share.

(*Yellow Bug!*)

TABLE OF CONTENTS

Fourth Week Scripture Reading (Sunday)   81

PREFACE

The story of Jesus's birth, as recounted in the Gospel of Luke, is at the heart of the Christian faith. It's a narrative that has been told and retold for two millennia, yet its power to inspire, comfort, and transform lives remains undiminished. *The Dawn of Hope* explores this timeless story, verse by verse, from Luke 2:1–52. Our journey will take us from the decree of Caesar Augustus to the boy Jesus in the Temple, examining each step of the way for its historical context, spiritual significance, and relevance to our lives today.

It has been a privilege to write about our dear Savior's birth. This stunning story never outstays its welcome and never loses its appeal. Both young and old, believers and seekers find immense joy in its retelling year after year. As I grew up in a Christian home, my parents read this remarkable story from Luke's Gospel to our family every Christmas, instilling in me a love for Luke's account.

In the Christmas narrative, we witness the unfolding of two incredibly divine mysteries: the Incarnation of our Lord Jesus Christ and his Virgin Birth. The word "Incarnation" comes from the Latin word *incarnatio*, which means "to be made flesh." It's derived from *in-*, meaning "into," and *caro* (stem "carn-"), meaning "flesh." So it means "the act of being made into flesh" or "taking on flesh." While the specific term "Incarnation" doesn't appear in the Bible, the concept of Jesus Christ (God) becoming a man is central to Christian doctrine and is based on several key passages: John 1:14, Philippians 2:6–8, Colossians 2:8–9, and 1 Timothy 3:16.

In the Christ child, Jesus, we see the God-man, eternally God, yet wholly man—the perfect Lamb of God who willingly gave up his life to *atone*[1] for our sins.

The Virgin Birth, as explained to Mary by the angel, was entirely God's doing: "The Holy Ghost shall come upon thee, and the power of the Highest shall overshadow thee: therefore, also that holy thing which shall be born of thee shall be called the Son of God" (Luke 1:35). Without the Virgin Birth, the Incarnation is impossible, and without the Incarnation, the Virgin Birth was unnecessary.

What Is Advent?

What is Advent, anyway? Advent is a season in many Christian church calendars, marking the beginning of the church year and spanning approximately four weeks leading up to Christmas. The term "Advent" derives from the Latin *Ad Venīre*, meaning "to come to" or "to arrive," reflecting the dual focus of this period: the anticipation of Christ's birth in Bethlehem and the expectation of his Second Coming at the end of time.

For those unfamiliar with this tradition, Advent is a time of preparation and reflection, inviting believers to pause amid the hustle of the holiday season and contemplate the profound mystery of the Incarnation.

Christians who deeply appreciate the Advent season often find in it a beautiful paradox: a time of quiet waiting filled with building excitement. It's a period when the soul is invited to both stillness and anticipation, mirroring the hushed expectancy of a world on the cusp of transformation. As carols begin to fill the air and festive decorations appear, those observing Advent cultivate an inner space of reflection, allowing the true meaning of Christmas to take root in their hearts. This season reminds believers that

---

1 To *atone* means to make up for wrongdoing, often by sacrificing something to make things right. This is what Jesus did for sinners. The Bible teaches, and Christians believe, that Jesus died on the cross to *atone* for humanity's sins. He paid for our sins.

just as the world once awaited a promised Savior, they also await his return, infusing the present moment with profound significance and joyful hope.

As an Advent book, *The Dawn of Hope* offers a day-by-day journey through Luke's account, providing a comprehensive and immersive experience. Unlike many Christmas-focused books, we delve into Jesus's early life beyond the Nativity, offering a broader perspective on the implications of his birth. Our approach interweaves scriptural analysis with practical applications, helping readers connect the ancient narrative to their daily lives.

After each chapter, you'll find a carefully chosen carol, hymn, or Gospel song that resonates with the chapter's themes. These sacred musical selections, ranging from beloved classics to lesser-known gems, are intended to deepen your reflection on the young Jesus and the hope his birth brings. As you read, I invite you to pause and consider these lyrical messages, allowing them to enrich your journey through the story and perhaps even inspire you to lift your own voice in song.

How to Use This Book

The Dawn of Hope is an Advent devotional whose entries are based entirely on chapter 2 of Luke's Gospel. I chose Luke's account for its uniquely detailed and chronological narrative of Jesus's birth and early life. Luke's medical background and attention to detail make his account vivid and relatable.

This book is intended for believers and those seeking the truth. Its pages are designed for believers to deepen their faith and rekindle their wonder at Christ's birth. For those seeking truth by exploring what the Bible says about the Lord Jesus, and what it teaches about his identity as the Son of God, I invite you to explore this narrative with an open heart. My desire is that you'll glimpse God's incredible love for you through this extraordinary story.

This book may be used by individuals in their personal quiet times, for family devotions, and small-group Bible studies. Let these chapters guide you through the four weeks of preparation for Christmas. The table of contents outlines Scripture readings and chapters for each week. On Sundays, read and meditate on the Scripture reading, which provides an overview of the week's content. For the following days of the week, read the narrative chapters based on Sunday's scripture. Each day's reading is designed to deepen your understanding of Jesus's early life and its relevance to your daily life.

The book is structured into twenty-four chapters, each focusing on a specific passage or theme from Luke's account. We'll meet a cast of characters, both divine and human—from Mary and Joseph to the shepherds and angels, from Simeon and Anna to Jesus himself. Along the way, we'll explore:

- The historical and cultural context of first-century Judea
- The theological implications of the Incarnation
- The human drama of the Nativity story
- The fulfillment of Old Testament prophecies[2]
- The relevance of these ancient events to our modern lives

Whether you're a seasoned Bible student, new to the Christian faith, or simply seeking "truth," I hope that this book will deepen your understanding and appreciation of the Advent story. As we journey together through these pages, may we all experience anew *the Dawn of Hope* that broke upon the world in a humble stable in Bethlehem.

I pray these glimpses into the Christmas story will help us live more like Jesus, revealing what God has done for us through the exciting people he used to tell this marvelous, life-changing story.

Let us begin our exploration with the decree that set everything in motion . . .

---

2 Prophecy, especially in the context of the Bible, is a message from God given to humans. It's God speaking to people through special messengers called prophets. These messages can be about events that would happen soon after they were given, events that would occur much later in history, the coming of Jesus (called the Messiah), or events that speak to what will happen at the end of the world. Fulfilled prophecies (the ones that came true already) prove that the Bible is reliable and that God keeps his promises. Many prophecies have already come true, while others are still waiting to happen.

ECHOES OF PROMISE

For centuries, whispers of hope had echoed through the hills of Judea and beyond. The Jewish people, heirs to a rich tapestry of prophecy, clung to the many promises of a coming Messiah in the Bible—a Savior who would *redeem*[3] not just Israel but all of humanity.

In the Garden of Eden,[4] as the first glimmers of this hope emerged even from among the consequences of mankind's first sin in Adam, God spoke of one who would bruise the serpent's head (Genesis 3:15). This seed of promise took root in the hearts of generations to come.

Through Abraham, the Lord declared, "And in thy seed shall all the nations of the earth be blessed" (Genesis 22:18). The expectation grew, a slender shoot reaching toward the light.

King David heard the astounding news that "thine house and thy kingdom shall be established for ever before thee: thy throne shall be

---

3   In Bible doctrine, "redeem" means to:

a. *Pay a price:* Jesus paid the price for humanity's sins through his death on the cross.

b. *Liberate or set free:* Jesus's sacrifice freed people from the bondage of sin and its eternal consequences.

c. *Restore:* The act of redemption restored the sinner's relationship with the Holy God, which was broken by sin.

d. *Reclaim ownership:* Jesus "bought back" humanity from the power of sin and death. Believers, remember, we were all slaves to sin until Jesus redeemed us!

4   The Garden of Eden refers to the paradise described in the Book of Genesis, the Bible's first book. This garden was the special home God made for his first-created people, Adam and Eve. It was a place of innocence and bliss before the introduction of sin into the world. Genesis 2:8 says, "And the LORD God planted a garden eastward in Eden, and there he put the man whom he had formed."

established for ever" (2 Samuel 7:16). The people began to dream of an eternal kingdom, just and righteous.

Isaiah's voice rang out, proclaiming, "For unto us a child is born, unto us a son is given: and the government shall be upon his shoulder: and his name shall be called Wonderful, Counsellor, The mighty God, The everlasting Father, The Prince of Peace" (Isaiah 9:6). The hope blossomed into vivid detail.

Micah pinpointed the humble birthplace: "But thou, Bethlehem Ephratah, though thou be little among the thousands of Judah, yet out of thee shall he come forth unto me that is to be ruler in Israel; whose goings forth have been from of old, from everlasting" (Micah 5:2).

Daniel spoke of timing, of weeks and years, kindling anticipation in scholarly minds (Daniel 9:24–26).

Zechariah painted a picture of a king: "Rejoice greatly, O daughter of Zion; shout, O daughter of Jerusalem: behold, thy King cometh unto thee: he is just, and having salvation; lowly, and riding upon [*a donkey*], and upon a colt the foal of [*a donkey*]" (Zechariah 9:9).

These prophecies and many more wove together, forming a tapestry of expectation. Generation after generation of Jews lived and died, holding these promises close to their hearts. They whispered them in the dark of night, taught them to their children, and clung to them in times of oppression and exile.

Rome's grip on ancient Israel tightened like a slowly closing fist. It began in 63 BCE, when Pompey's legions marched into Jerusalem, planting the seeds of Roman influence. The soil of control was further tilled in 37 BCE, as Herod the Great, a Roman puppet, ascended to the throne. By 6 CE, Rome's dominion bloomed fully—the once-independent land now neatly labeled and managed as the Roman province of Judea. In less than seven decades, a proud kingdom had become another jewel in Rome's vast imperial crown.[5]

---

5 Roman Rule in Israel was from 63 BCE to 313 CE, according to the Jewish Virtual Library, date: August 15, 2024, from: https://www.jewishvirtuallibrary.org/roman-rule-63bce-313ce.

Now, in 3 BCE, Roman power held sway over Judea. The longing for the Messiah burned brighter than ever. In synagogues and homes, in fields and marketplaces, the questions hung in the air: "When will he come? How shall we recognize him?"

Little did they know that events were already in motion in the small town of Nazareth. The stage was set, the actors were in place, and the greatest story ever told was about to unfold. The Word was about to become flesh,[6] and hope itself would take human form.

It was into this world of ancient promises and fervent expectations that a decree went out from Caesar Augustus . . .

---

6 This phrase is pointing to Jesus "the Word," becoming a man "the flesh." It is another way of saying "the Incarnation."

First Week Scripture Reading (Sunday)

And it came to pass in those days, that there went out a decree from Caesar Augustus, that all the world should be taxed. (And this taxing was first made when Cyrenius was governor of Syria.) And all went to be taxed, every one into his own city. And Joseph also went up from Galilee, out of the city of Nazareth, into Judaea, unto the city of David, which is called Beth-lehem; (because he was of the house and lineage of David:) To be taxed with Mary his espoused wife, being great with child.

And so it was, that, while they were there, the days were accomplished that she should be delivered. And she brought forth her firstborn son, and wrapped him in swaddling clothes, and laid him in a manger; because there was no room for them in the inn.

And there were in the same country shepherds abiding in the field, keeping watch over their flock by night. And, lo, the angel of the Lord came upon them, and the glory of the Lord shone round about them: and they were sore afraid. And the angel said unto them, Fear not: for, behold, I bring you good tidings of great joy, which shall be to all people. For unto you is born this day in the city of David a Savior, which is Christ the Lord. And this shall be a sign unto you; Ye shall find the babe wrapped in swaddling clothes, lying in a manger. And suddenly there was with the angel a multitude of the heavenly host praising God, and saying,

Glory to God in the highest,

And on earth peace,

Good will toward men.

—Luke 2:1–14

CHAPTER 1

THE DECREE—LUKE 2:1–3 (WEEK 1, MONDAY)

The air was thick with hopelessness in the villages dotting the rugged terrain. The once-vibrant faith of the Israelites had been eroded by decades of foreign occupation. The people's spirits were worn down by the relentless cycle of tyranny and conquest.

Jerusalem itself, the crown jewel that had once shone as a beacon of faith, saw its sacred places profaned by the presence of pagan idols and Roman standards. Resentment was stiff as the Jewish people seethed at the sacrilegious encroachment on their Holy City and way of life. Even the high priests, who were meant to tend to the spiritual needs of the people, found their activities dictated by the will of their foreign overlords.

For the devout Jews, this oppression represented not only a political humiliation but a defilement of their covenant with the One True God. The pagans who now ruled over them erected idols and statues of false deities in the very land Yahweh had promised as an eternal inheritance. This sent a chill of despair through the populace, who saw their holy Temple overshadowed by the might of Rome.

The Pax Romana, or "Roman Peace," was a time when the mighty Roman Empire claimed to bring peace to its vast lands. But for many people living under Roman rule, this "peace" felt more like chains. While Rome's cities gleamed with marble and gold, its conquered territories often suffered under the weight of heavy taxes and strict laws. The empire's idea of peace meant crushing rebellions and silencing those who disagreed, showing that true peace involves more than just the absence of war.

Each new mandate from the imperial city seemed more crushing than the last. The Roman occupation had become a yoke that chafed and bent the back of the Jewish people lower with every passing year. Any murmurings of resistance were swiftly crushed underfoot by the mighty Roman forces, who showed no restraint in their brutality toward dissent. The land of Israel groaned under the weight of the pagan armies.

Despair had settled over the land, and the air was laced with misery. Burdened by excessive taxes demanded by their Roman masters, even the most diligent struggled to put bread on the table. Some citizens were reduced to begging for scraps that the Roman soldiers' horses had passed over. Many went hungry. The oppressive yoke weighed heavily upon them, crushing spirits and killing dreams.

The general population lived in fear, feeling abandoned by the Almighty as pagan cruelties mounted. But even with no deliverer in sight, God's faithful continued to tend to the flickering flame of hope that Rome threatened to extinguish.

After many long years of suffering and darkness, hope finally pierced through the gloom. It arrived humbly and unexpectedly: a tiny baby lying in a simple manger. This seemingly ordinary, lowly child was the promised Savior people had been waiting for. He was the One who would blaze a trail of light to overcome the sin, oppression, and despair that had smothered the world for so long. His coming would change everything, setting humanity on an entirely new course.

But don't let me get too far ahead of the story. The emergence of this great hope began under the most unfavorable circumstances you can imagine in this weary, troubled world. The night had been long, but *the Dawn of Hope* was about to rise . . .

In the days when Caesar Augustus held dominion over the vast Roman Empire, a new decree was made that sent ripples through the known world.

With an empire extending from the Western Mediterranean to the far reaches of the East, the mighty Caesar commanded that a census be taken. This was not merely an administrative act but a far-reaching proclamation that would shape the destinies of those dwelling in the far corners of the known world.

The edict resounded with the authority of Caesar Augustus: *"And it came to pass in those days that there went out a decree from Caesar Augustus, that all the world[7] should be taxed. (And this taxing was first made when Cyrenius was governor of Syria.) And all went to be taxed, every one into his own city"* (Luke 2:1–3).

The effects of this decree were earthshaking. It was a proclamation that reached into the lives of ordinary people, disrupting their routines and, in many cases, compelling them to undertake journeys to their ancestral homes.

The world was set in motion, not by the wheels of chariots or the might of armies, but by a few quill strokes on a parchment. Families, from the bustling cities to the quiet villages, were summoned to return to the places of their lineage, a call echoing through the hills and plains.

For Joseph, a carpenter by trade, and Mary, his betrothed wife, this meant a pilgrimage of seven to ten days or longer to Bethlehem, the city of David. It meant traversing ninety to one hundred miles[8] of dusty roads and navigating the terrain with a purpose far surpassing the mundane act of registration or collecting a few more coins in taxes. It was a journey not of their choosing but one ordained by the Almighty Father, setting the stage for the unfolding drama of the Incarnation.

---

7 The "world" here speaks of the known world under Rome's authority.

8 This was about 90 to 100 miles or 145 to 160 kilometers. The couple could likely travel 10 to 15 miles (16 to 24 kilometers) a day at the most. Remember the terrain, hilly areas, and valleys to traverse. Mary's advanced pregnancy would have slowed their pace significantly. They would need frequent stops for rest, food, and water. Even with the use of a donkey carrying supplies, or Mary, their speed would not have increased much.

To the world, this decree represented the exercise of imperial authority, a testament to the magnitude of Caesar's rule. It was a reminder that even in the empire's quiet corners, Caesar's decree could penetrate, reshaping lives and histories. It marked an era when the political plotting of the powerful had tangible and far-reaching consequences for the common folk.

The mandate was but a single thread in the grand tapestry of history. Yet it wove together the elaborate patterns of God's providence. Little did the earth's rulers realize that God's divine plan was set into motion within the mundane act of counting heads for taxation. Unaware of the imminent miracle, the world continued its rhythm, oblivious to the enormous significance of a pregnant maiden and a carpenter on a journey. Caesar's seemingly arbitrary command became the instrument to fulfill ancient prophecies. It brought to light the merging of divine sovereignty over human history. In the quiet obedience of Mary and Joseph, the stage was being prepared for the entrance of a child whose birth would transform the course of humanity's future.

"Ye dwellers in darkness with sin-blinded eyes,
The Light of the world is Jesus!
Go, wash at His bidding, and light will arise;
The Light of the world is Jesus!

Come to the light, 'tis shining for thee;
Sweetly, the light has dawned upon me;
Once, I was blind, but now I can see:
The Light of the world is Jesus!"[9]

---

9   "The Light of the World is Jesus," by Philip P. Bliss (1875), the third verse and refrain. Copyright Status: public domain.

CHAPTER 2

THE JOURNEY—LUKE 2:4-5 (TUESDAY)

Joseph and Mary's trip to Bethlehem was no ordinary journey. It was a world-changing event carefully planned by God. Their travels set the stage for a miracle that would give mankind an opportunity for eternal life. It will bring new hope to humanity: *"And Joseph also went up from Galilee, out of the city of Nazareth, into Judaea, unto the city of David, which is called Bethlehem; (because he was of the house and lineage of David:) To be taxed with Mary his espoused wife, being great with child"* (Luke 2:4–5).

Joseph looked at Mary with concern. She was very pregnant, and the baby could come any day now. The long trip to Bethlehem worried him. Joseph got a small donkey for her to ride to make things easier for Mary. They packed only what they needed: food, extra clothes, and warm blankets. Even though the journey seemed uncertain, they trusted God to keep them safe and show them the way. Their faith gave them courage for the hard road ahead.

The dusty road stretched endlessly before them under the scorching Judean sun. Joseph glanced over at Mary, her delicate frame made more prominent by the precious child growing within her. Though this miraculous pregnancy bowed her shoulders, determination etched lines on her serene face. They were starting on a long, hard trip. Joseph was a simple carpenter, but he came from the family of King David. So he had to travel from his home in Nazareth in Galilee, to Bethlehem, King David's city in Judea. Augustus Caesar didn't know it, but his order actually helped God's amazing plan come true. Long ago, the prophet Micah had predicted that the promised Savior would be born in Bethlehem. God was using the emperor's command to make this happen—an event that would change the world forever.

Mary, engaged to marry Joseph, was pregnant with a very special baby. This wasn't just any child—it was the Messiah[10] for whom the people had been waiting for hundreds of years. Mary's pregnancy was a miracle. She hadn't been with any man; God's Holy Spirit had made this baby grow inside her.

The young couple didn't fully understand that by following the emperor's order, they were part of God's big plan. God, the great I AM who rules over everything, was using this human law to fulfill his promises. He was arranging all the details to fit his special plan.

Inside Mary was God's greatest gift from heaven—a baby who was both God and human. This was the Messiah, God's own Son, sent to save the world. Every step of their journey brought this amazing miracle closer to happening.

They left Nazareth as the sun rose that morning, its golden rays peeking over the Galilean hills. The road stretched endlessly before them, a dusty serpent slithering toward Judea. Mary rode the donkey, her swollen belly preceding her frail body. Joseph walked alongside, a steady hand on the donkey's bridle.

The first few days moved slowly, Joseph keeping a measured pace so as not to exhaust Mary or the donkey. Poor Mary endured suffering indeed, her belly protruding as the donkey's steady sways jostled her tender frame. Joseph glanced at Mary with concern, her delicate form weighed down by the miraculous child growing within her. Her weariness showed on her face, but an unmistakable strength and resilience burned in her eyes. When her back ached from the constant swaying, they would stop to rest in the shade. Joseph tenderly massaged her ankles, which had ballooned

---

10 Messiah: In biblical terms, the Savior or Liberator chosen by God to deliver people from sin or oppression. The Messiah is "the Christ" or the "Anointed One" by God the Father. Jesus Christ is the Messiah.

during the day's travels. This devout couple trusted God's divine plan to guide every plodding step of their journey.

Each night brought deepening shadows over the path, and the temperatures plunged. They huddled under the starry expanse, the donkey's brays piercing the stillness. Sleeping on the hard ground couldn't have been easy for Mary. Joseph saw to her comfort as best he could, though in these circumstances, it amounted to little more than a thin mat and rough-spun blanket. She never grumbled, but he could see the strain on her face as she slept. The friendly beast's soft whinnies and brays formed a calming air as Joseph kept vigil over Mary while she slumbered. His heart swelled with awe at being entrusted as the earthly "dad" to the promised King. Each miracle—from the angel's proclamation to the child's divine conception—seemed too wondrous to comprehend. Yet by faith, he believed every angelic word. God's perfect plan was unfolding with every step of their journey. Joseph and Mary, humble and faithful, unknowingly became God's instruments in a worldwide narrative.

Each morning, they arose tired but determined, packing their few belongings to follow the path. As Joseph tenderly helped his betrothed onto the back of their donkey, he whispered hushed prayers for her comfort and the child's protection. The beast's rhythmic clops provided a modest cadence to mark their progress.

The dry air in the valleys between hilltop towns was hot and thick, making each breath labored. Shepherd boys offered them waterskins from cold mountain streams, relieving their cracked lips and parched throats. They graciously accepted the kind villagers' provisions—figs, olives, lentil stew. Some days, the congested roads slowed their pace to a crawl as scores of others fled to their ancestral lands to be counted. But no delay was too wearying, no discomfort too unbearable when eternity's purpose propelled them onward. Mary did not utter a word of complaint. She moved with quiet resilience, trusting that the Almighty went before them, ordaining each circumstance according to his perfect will.

Joseph glanced at her. "Are you all right, Mary?" he asked with concern, reaching over to steady her as she swayed slightly on the back of the donkey. "We can rest whenever you need to."

Mary gave him a weary but grateful smile. "I am well, Joseph. The child within me grows restless, but we must keep moving on."

Though the journey was exhausting, heaven's miraculous plan was in full motion through this young couple's faithfulness. All creation paused in awe of the sacred event that was about to occur. The miracle of the Christ child's birth was imminent.

Finally, after nearly two weeks of travel, they crested a hill, and there in the afternoon sun was David's City. The weary couple caught sight of Bethlehem in the distance—a humble cluster of simple dwellings presided over by an aging stone watchtower. Joseph quickened, anxious to reach their destination before Mary began her labor. He uttered a prayer of thanks that they had arrived safely in the ancient city of his ancestors.

As the husband and dad-to-be, Joseph's responsibilities weighed heavily. Providing shelter and safety for his little family was paramount. But how could he secure proper lodging in Bethlehem when the town was overflowing with travelers facing the same imperial decree? Joseph uttered a silent prayer for strength and guidance from the Almighty. Mary sensed her husband's worries. Though her weariness bowed her shoulders, she squeezed his arm reassuringly. After their shock at the miraculous news of her pregnancy, they resigned to following wherever God led, even into this humanly impossible situation. The favor of the Lord rested on them—of this, they were assured.

When they entered the city gates, the crowd's din assaulted them— strident haggling, animals lowing, the reedy wails of restless babies. The air hung heavy with smoky dust and the dank smell of sweat. Overwhelmed by fatigue and her condition, Mary wobbled in the saddle. "Joseph . . . " she breathed, one hand cradling her belly. Renewed determination surged through him. Looping the donkey's reins over his arm, Joseph forged a path through the churning masses, seeking anyone to offer a room, stable, or hovel where his betrothed could have the child in privacy and safety. Amid the clamor, the impending birth of this child held universal significance. Unrecognized by the world, God's promise would be fulfilled in the humblest of settings. The very heartbeat of God would soon echo in the cries of a newborn, and the course of human redemption would be forever altered. Unaware of the unfolding miracle, the world carried on with its daily routines, yet the foundations of eternity were laid beneath the surface.

As the world slept that night, oblivious to the celestial drama unfolding, Joseph and Mary's exhausting journey ended in Bethlehem. The stage was now set for the birth of the Christ child, who would transform the world and offer salvation to mankind.

"O little town of Bethlehem,
how still we see thee lie!
Above thy deep and dreamless sleep,
the silent stars go by.
Yet in thy dark streets shineth
the everlasting light;
the hopes and fears of all the years
are met in thee tonight."[11]

---

11 "O Little Town of Bethlehem," by Philips Brooks (1868), the first verse. Public domain.

CHAPTER 3

THE STABLE—LUKE 2:7 (WEDNESDAY)

In the quaint village of Bethlehem, a crucial event was about to unfold. The whispers of the breeze carried the hopes and dreams of a people eagerly awaiting the arrival of the promised Savior.[12] The heavens seemed to hold their breath in anticipation as a young couple, their faces looking tired but hopeful, sought shelter in a humble stall.

The night's contrast between the village events and the birth-hut activities was stark! While the town was bustling with people due to the census, they were unaware of the momentous event developing in a stable yards away. The text vividly portrays a humble stable, filled with the earthy scents of hay and animals, where the most extraordinary event in human history was taking place, a scene that would forever change the course of humanity: *"And she brought forth her firstborn son and wrapped him in swaddling clothes and laid him in a manger because there was no room for them in the inn"* (Luke 2:7).

That night, Mary and Joseph must have felt deep worry and amazement. They found themselves in less-than-ideal circumstances—they were far from home, without proper lodging, and about to experience childbirth in a stable. Yet they were also about to see God's promise come true right before their eyes.

---

12 A Savior is someone who rescues people from danger or harm. In the Bible, Jesus is called the Savior because he saves people from their sins and the punishment those sins deserve. Jesus died on the cross to take the punishment for people's wrongdoings (sin) so they can be forgiven and have a relationship with God.

Picture the scene: a simple stable, its warped wooden walls and drooping roof worn by time. The air is filled with the smell of hay; the only sounds are the soft rustling of animals and the occasional distant sheep bleating. In this humble shelter, Mary, tired yet glowing, cradles her newborn son. Joseph, the carpenter turned guardian, watches over them both.

"But this picture, it seems all wrong!" Our hearts cry out. "No room? A stable is no fit place for the King of kings to be born!" Our hearts are torn between anger at the injustice and wonder at the miracle unfolding. No grand palace, no beautiful rooms, only a poor stable with a manger turned into a makeshift crib! Yet the importance of this simple stable, chosen by God, can't be overstated. In this humble setting, the King of kings chose to enter the world, which surprised everyone and showed us his willingness to be born in the simplest of places.

The effects of Jesus's birth in a stable, rather than a palace, are as meaningful as they are poetic. The contrast between earthly circumstances and divine significance is stark, and it speaks to the heart of the Savior's mission. Choosing a stable challenges the idea of earthly glory in a world that loves luxury and power. It goes against what we expect of a King, showing a different kind of kingdom—based on humility and selfless love, not worldly standards.

A palace might have shown authority, but a stable shows that Jesus will be easy to approach. In this simple setting, the Savior reveals his willingness to meet humanity at its most basic level, bridging the gap between the divine and the ordinary. In the birth of Jesus, God reached out his hand to a world trapped in the cycle of sin and suffering. Through Jesus, there will be a new beginning, a way of forgiveness,[13] and a fresh start for humanity. With its earthy scents and humble surroundings, the stable proves God's willingness to meet us where we are in our sins. This

---

13 In the Bible, forgiveness is about God removing the guilt of our sins (bad things we do, think, or say) and not holding them against us anymore. When the Bible talks about being "forgiven," it means that God has wiped away our sins because of Jesus, and we're no longer in trouble with God for our sin.

was a place of inclusion, where the lowly and the mighty, the rich and the poor, all may find common ground at the foot of a manger.

God's choice of place for this humble birth challenges what the world values. It teaches us that true greatness is found not in riches and power but in helping others in their struggles. The stable becomes a sanctuary of grace, reminding us that the essence of God's love is not confined to the grandeur of palaces but flourishes in the simplicity of hearts surrendered to him.

As we reflect on the humble stable in Bethlehem, we find ourselves encouraged to lay down our ambitions for earthly glory and kneel before the gracious Savior instead. In this meek birthplace, the world's Savior extends an invitation to a kingdom where the humble are exalted, the broken are made whole, and the simplicity of a stable becomes the gateway to the King! In essence, the moment of Jesus's birth brought bright hope to the world and created a radical change in the relationship between the Creator and his creatures. However, its full impact would only be realized in the years to come.

"Away in a manger, no crib for a bed,
The little Lord Jesus laid down His sweet head.
The stars in the heavens looked down where He lay,
the little Lord Jesus asleep on the hay."[14]

---

14 "Away in a Manger," (attributed to) Martin Luther, first stanza. Copyright: public domain.

CHAPTER 4

THE INCARNATION—LUKE 2:6–7 (THURSDAY)

Under the starry sky, something miraculous was about to happen in the quiet town of Bethlehem. This small place, known as the city of David,[15] lay tucked away in the gentle hills of Judea. A helpless baby was about to be born, one who would touch the hearts of all people searching for help and hope. It's hard to believe, but this tiny Savior would determine eternity for every person. The simple yet beautiful words of the Bible tell us about this incredible moment when God's Son, Jesus, came to earth in human flesh:[16] *"And so it was, that, while they were there, the days were accomplished that she should be delivered. And she brought forth her firstborn son, and wrapped him in swaddling clothes, and laid him in a manger; because there was no room for them in the inn"* (Luke 2:6–7).

Imagine the scene: a humble stable becomes the sacred place where God meets humanity. The night air is cool and still, as if all creation is holding its breath. Our Creator, the Messiah, the Son of God, takes his first breath as a human baby. Mary, chosen by God as Jesus's mother, holds

---

15 In the sunbaked hills of Judea, Bethlehem cradled the roots of a royal legacy. Here, Jesse raised his son David, who grew from a humble shepherd boy into Israel's greatest king. The town's dusty streets witnessed young David's adventures before he was chosen to lead. Years later, the prophet Micah pointed to Bethlehem as the future birthplace of the promised Savior. When Jesus was born there, it wove another golden thread into the town's rich tapestry, forever linking it to King David's name.

16 "Incarnation": literally, "in the flesh." Jesus Christ, the Son of God, has come to live among humans in a body of flesh and blood.

the long-awaited Savior in her arms. The only sounds are the soft lowing of cattle and the quiet rustling of straw.

Luke's words show us how unique this birth was, even in such an ordinary place. He wasn't just any baby[17]—this was Jesus Christ, the King of kings. Yet he didn't arrive in a grand castle or a fancy hospital. Instead, he came in the hush of night, in a simple stable that didn't even belong to his family. The swaddling clothes weren't royal robes but simple strips of cloth. And his first bed? A borrowed manger—used to feed animals, now cradling the One who would feed our souls. Jesus's humble birth shows that he came to serve and save everyone. He came not as a distant ruler but as the Good Shepherd,[18] ready to care for and save *all* who would follow him.

The birth of Jesus Christ was not an isolated event. God had been planning it since before he laid the foundation of the world! He told people about it hundreds of years before it happened. This is what we call prophecy. About seven hundred years before Jesus was born, God spoke through a prophet named Isaiah, who wrote: "The Lord himself will give you a sign: A virgin will become pregnant and have a son and will name Him Immanuel" (Isaiah 7:14, paraphrased).

This prophecy tells us something very important: Jesus would be born to a virgin. This means his mother, Mary, had never been with a man when

---

17 This baby was Jesus Christ Incarnate. The Incarnation happened when the all-powerful, all-knowing God chose to become a real human being. It was the Creator, Jesus, of the entire universe being born as a baby into his creation and living on earth as one of us, while still remaining God at the same time.

18 The Good Shepherd is a name used for Jesus Christ. It comes from the Bible, specifically John chapter 10. In this part of the Bible, Jesus describes himself as a shepherd who takes care of and protects his flock of sheep. The sheep represent his followers or believers. This name shows how Jesus cares for and guides those who follow him, as a shepherd looks after his sheep.

she became pregnant with Jesus. Instead, the Holy Spirit of God made this miracle happen.[19]

Later, when Jesus was about to be born, God reminded people of this prophecy. In the book of Matthew in the New Testament, we read that God spoke to Joseph in a dream to say that he would become Jesus's earthly father. Hearkening back to Isaiah's words, God told Joseph: "The virgin will conceive and give birth to a son, and they will call Him Immanuel ('God with us')" (Matthew 1:23, paraphrased).[20]

This prophecy shows us that Jesus's birth was an astonishing event. And the name "Immanuel" tells us something miraculous—that in Jesus, God himself was coming to live with people like us!

The Virgin Birth of Jesus is a lighthouse guiding us through the stormy seas of human history. It is significant because it shows us that Jesus is fully God and fully human. Being born to a virgin means Jesus came into the world without sin. This miraculous conception is vital for three key reasons:

1. **It is a fulfilled prophecy.** In Isaiah 7:14, God said, "Therefore the Lord himself shall give you a sign; Behold, a virgin shall conceive, and bear a son, and shall call his name Immanuel." This shows us God's faithfulness. He promised and fulfilled his promise. The Bible is true. The Virgin Birth validates Jesus's identity as the Messiah.

2. **Jesus's Virgin Birth breaks the chain of inherited sin from Adam.** Sin entered the world through Adam's disobedience to God in the Garden of Eden. God held Adam, as the representative of humanity, responsible for this fall. As a result, all humans born through natural procreation inherit Adam's sinful nature. By being born of a virgin, Jesus did not inherit the sinful nature

---

19 "Virgin Birth"—Jesus was conceived and born of the Virgin Mary. At the time of His conception, development in her womb, and birth, she was a virgin without the involvement of a human father. The Holy Spirit caused this miraculous conception.
20 Read Matthew 1:18–25 for the full encounter in Joseph's dream.

that is passed down through human fathers. This ensures Jesus's qualification as the perfect sacrifice for our sin. He is the "sinless Savior" of humanity.

3. **Jesus is God incarnate as Man.** The Virgin Birth allows Jesus to be fully God and fully human. It bridges the gap between his divinity and his humanity, making possible Jesus's unique role as the mediator between God and Man.

As one of my wife's first graders said, "The Incarnation is when God got dressed up in a man." The Bible says, "The Word [*Jesus*] was made flesh." Christ came into our broken world to bridge the gap that our sin had made between God and sinners. His birth was God's loving intervention to rescue us from the darkness of sin and restore our broken fellowship with him. His story will climax with his death on the cross for all sin. But that is not the end of the story. He will be buried and rise from the dead on the third day. His resurrected life will justify each believing sinner. Jesus offers to all forgiveness and eternal life. He will freely give salvation to anyone who believes in him and trusts his sacrifice for their sin.

This Advent, let's ponder the amazing truth of the Incarnation. Only in Jesus Christ do we have hope for this life and the next.

"Christ, by highest heaven adored,
Christ, the everlasting Lord,
late in time behold Him come,
offspring of the Virgin's womb:
veiled in flesh, the Godhead see;
hail [*the incarnate*][21] Deity,
pleased with us in flesh to dwell,
Jesus, our Immanuel."[22]

---

21 The wording was changed slightly for singing; "the incarnate" was sung "th'incarnate."
22 "Hark! the Herald Angels Sing," by Charles Wesley (1739), second verse. Alterer: George Whitefield. Public domain.

CHAPTER 5

THE SHEPHERDS—LUKE 2:8 (FRIDAY)

A group of shepherds carefully watched their sheep in the peaceful countryside near Bethlehem, where gentle hills met the starry night sky. In a world that often ignored ordinary people and thought simple things were unimportant, these lowly shepherds were about to receive a fantastic message they would be compelled to share with others.

The moon hung low, casting a soft light over the hills. The Bible tells the heavenly story: *"And there were in the same country shepherds abiding in the field, keeping watch over their flock by night"* (Luke 2:8).

These simple words carry significant meanings that have lasted throughout time.

Picture the shepherds in their old, worn, dirt-covered robes, their faces weather-beaten and hands rough from hard work. On this quiet night, on that lonely hill, the small flame and sooty smoke of their campfire illustrated the lowliness of their occupation. But right here, God's story was about to take a surprising turn.

A shepherd's life was filled with repetitive tasks. Day after day, night after night, they looked after their sheep. It seemed like their lives didn't matter much in the big scheme of life. They felt the heaviness of being at the bottom of society, constantly reminded that they weren't important to others. Their random yawns and tired eyes reflected their nights of watching their flocks.

In the quiet night, the shepherds gathered around their small campfire. Its flames barely lit up the darkness around them. The smoke made their eyes water, a familiar discomfort in their dull routine. They shared old bread and watery wine, and their meager rations were very different from the food enjoyed by the rich and powerful. They didn't talk much, with long silences broken only by the soft baas of sheep and the gentle sound of wind in the grass.

As they gazed at the vast, starry sky, the shepherds might have wondered if their lives would ever be more than just tending these Temple sheep. Would anyone remember them? Would their lives matter beyond these hills? Little did they know that their seemingly ordinary lives were about to intertwine with God's extraordinary plan,[23] forever changing the course of history.

God had a surprising plan for this world. He chose to reveal his greatest secret not to kings or queens but to humble shepherds. With rough hands and weathered faces, these simple men were about to hear the most important news in history—the angelic announcement of the birth of Jesus, the Savior.

The stage was set for something truly remarkable. While the powerful and wealthy busied themselves with their own affairs, God was quietly preparing to speak to ordinary shepherds. This unexpected choice showed how God often works in surprising ways.

As the night grew later, a feeling of expectation hung in the air like a whisper from heaven. Not knowing an amazing event was about to happen, the shepherds kept watching their sheep in the quiet fields near Bethlehem. Very soon, their ordinary night would become extraordinary, and these humble shepherds would become the bearers of a message of hope echoing through eternity.

"If you take good heed to the angel's words;
Rise up, shepherd, and follow;
You'll forget your flocks, you'll forget your herds;
Rise up, shepherd, and follow."[24]

---

23 God, the Creator and Sovereign of the universe, has meticulously planned all of existence from the beginning of time. He has a plan for each one in his creation.

24 "Rise Up, Shepherds, and Follow," Traditional Spiritual, third verse. Copyright: public domain.

CHAPTER 6

THE ANGELS—LUKE 2:9–14 (SATURDAY)

Bethlehem was quiet under the night sky. The shepherds in the nearby fields were used to watching their sheep in the dark. But this night would be different. Suddenly, a light brighter than anything they'd ever seen split the sky. An angel with glowing wings appeared before them! They knew they were about to hear something important from heaven.

The ancient sacred words came alive on this heavenly stage:

And, lo, the angel of the Lord came upon them, and the glory of the Lord shone round about them: and they were sore afraid. And the angel said unto them, "Fear not: for, behold, I bring you good tidings of great joy, which shall be to all people. For unto you is born this day in the city of David a Savior, which is Christ the Lord. And this shall be a sign unto you; Ye shall find the babe wrapped in swaddling clothes, lying in a manger." And suddenly there was with the angel a multitude of the heavenly host praising God, and saying,

"Glory to God in the highest,

And on earth, peace,

Good will toward men." (Luke 2:9–14)

Picture this: The shepherds were watching their sheep. Unexpectedly, they were bathed in bright, heavenly light. An angel stood before them. Their hearts raced, and their legs shook. The men fell to the ground in fear. They had never seen anything like this before. The angel, God's messenger, was about to give them the most important news the world would ever hear.

The first thing the angel said was, "Do not be afraid." These words were like a healing balm for humanity's souls. The sky itself seemed to sigh with relief. This announcement was not just for a few shepherds in some faraway field. This was a message of hope for all of us. The entire world needs to be saved and restored to fellowship with God. With Jesus, all fear is taken out of the equation for those who believe this message.

A multitude of angels filled the sky with songs of praise. Their celestial voices proclaimed the Savior's arrival. The heavens, which had seen all of creation unfold, now shouted the most crucial part of God's plan—*Christ, the promised Messiah, has finally come to earth!*

The angels' message pierced the darkness of the sinful world. This message of hope offered all humanity a promise of peace. God's glory, hidden for so long, now shone brightly. This message meant everyone was now invited to accept God's love, like a bridge connecting heaven and earth. The birth of the Savior in a simple stable was more important than anyone could have imagined. It was an event of eternal significance.

As the angels retreated into heaven, their songs echoed in the shepherds' hearts and would be remembered for as long as they lived. In that holy moment, heaven touched the earth, and a spark of hope burst into a bright flame. This light would shine through this world's darkness for all time.

"Hark! The herald angels sing,
'Glory to the newborn King:
peace on earth, and mercy mild,
God and sinners reconciled!'
Joyful, all ye nations, rise,
join the triumph of the skies;
with th'angelic hosts proclaim,
'Christ is born in Bethlehem!'
Hark! The herald angels sing,
'Glory to the newborn King.'"[25]

---

25 "Hark! the Herald Angels Sing," by Charles Wesley (1739), first verse and refrain. Alterer: George Whitefield. Public domain.

Second Week Scripture Reading (Sunday)

And it came to pass, as the angels were gone away from them into heaven, the shepherds said one to another, "Let us now go even unto Beth-lehem, and see this thing which is come to pass, which the Lord hath made known unto us." And they came with haste, and found Mary, and Joseph, and the babe lying in a manger.

And when they had seen it, they made known abroad the saying which was told them concerning this child. And all they that heard it wondered at those things which were told them by the shepherds. But Mary kept all these things, and pondered them in her heart. And the shepherds returned, glorifying and praising God for all the things that they had heard and seen, as it was told unto them.

And when eight days were accomplished for the circumcising of the child, his name was called JESUS, which was so named of the angel before he was conceived in the womb.

And when the days of her purification according to the law of Moses were accomplished, they brought him to Jerusalem, to present him to the Lord; (As it is written in the law of the Lord, "Every male that openeth the womb shall be called holy to the Lord;") And to offer a sacrifice according to that which is said in the law of the Lord, "A pair of turtledoves, or two young pigeons."

And, behold, there was a man in Jerusalem, whose name was Simeon; and the same man was just and devout, waiting for the consolation of Israel: and the Holy Ghost was upon him. And it was revealed unto him by the Holy Ghost, that he should not see death, before he had seen the Lord's Christ. And he came by the Spirit into the temple: and when the parents brought in the child Jesus, to do for him after the custom of the law.

—Luke 2:15–27

CHAPTER 7

THE ADORATION—LUKE 2:15-16 (MONDAY)

And it came to pass, as the angels were gone away from them into heaven, the shepherds said one to another, "Let us now go even unto Bethlehem, and see this thing which is come to pass, which the Lord hath made known unto us." And they came with haste and found Mary, and Joseph, and the babe lying in a manger.

—Luke 2:15–16

The shepherds were transfixed, their faces aglow in the fading heavenly light. The incredible spectacle they had just witnessed left them speechless. An angel had told them the fantastic news—the Savior was born in Bethlehem!

Their sheep huddled together in the fields, unaware of the surprising events around them. The beautiful song of the angels still seemed to float in the cool night air, making the shepherds want to hurry to Bethlehem. They knew they would find the baby that God had promised long ago.

The angel's words echoed in the men's minds, guiding them like a map from heaven—a map that would lead them to the stable where the newborn Savior awaited.

So these humble shepherds set out on their journey. A cool breeze carried the scents of wild herbs and distant sheep, mingling with the earthy smell of the dusty road. In the distance, they could hear the faint barking of village dogs and the soft rustling of olive trees. The night air felt crisp against their skin, invigorating them as they hurried toward Bethlehem.

The road was uneven and hard to see at night, but a strange, beautiful star illuminated their way. The brightness made their shadows dance as they walked quickly along the path. With each step, the men felt more and more confident they were part of something divine. Yes, they were no longer just watching their sheep—they were on their way to see the promised Messiah!

When they arrived at the stable, they quietly stopped at the entrance. Joseph stepped forward protectively. His brow furrowed with caution and curiosity. Still resting from childbirth, Mary raised her head, her eyes reflecting a quiet strength and wonder at these unexpected visitors.

As the shepherds stepped in, they were enveloped by the warmth of animals and the pungent scent of the stable. The air hung thick with the smell of livestock and the sweet aroma of fresh straw. Soft coos and gentle bleats from nearby animals created a soothing backdrop.

Their eyes were drawn by the soft glow of a lamp that shone on baby Jesus, sleeping in a rough cradle. There he was. This tiny baby was the one God had promised long ago. They could hardly believe their eyes—here was the newborn Son of God! They saw exactly what the angels had told them: the King of kings, wrapped in cloth strips, lying in a manger.

As they reverently beheld the child, the men realized something important: They were not just observers but a part of God's eternal plan! They each humbly knelt on the rough floor.

Each man sensed God's love and purpose. They realized that in choosing them—simple shepherds—to witness this moment, God showed that his love and salvation were for all people, regardless of their past or status.

These rugged men, who usually called out loudly to their sheep, now softly sang praises to the baby. Their hearts were full, and their gratitude filled the stable.

Joseph's posture relaxed as he placed a comforting hand on Mary's shoulder, their eyes meeting in a moment of shared awe and understanding. Mary winked knowingly and smiled broadly at Joseph, gently stroking Jesus's tiny hand.

Baby Jesus seemed to know what was happening. He looked at these shepherds who had hurried to meet *him*. These were just ordinary working men, but now they were part of something extraordinary. They were gladdened by the child before them—they had seen the face of God in this newborn, and in that face, they saw *the Dawn of Hope* for all humankind.

"What Child is this, who laid to rest,
On Mary's lap is sleeping?
Whom angels greet with anthems sweet,
While shepherds watch are keeping?

This, this is Christ, the King,
Whom shepherds guard and angels sing:
Haste, haste to bring Him laud,
The Babe, the Son of Mary!"[26]

---

26 "What Child Is This," by W. Chatterton Dix, first verse and chorus. Public domain.

CHAPTER 8

THE WITNESSES—LUKE 2:17–18, 20 (TUESDAY)

After worshiping baby Jesus, the shepherds were filled with a tremendous sense of awe, joy, and thankfulness. They were deeply moved to be the first to receive this tremendous news. They said to each other, "God has revealed to us this amazing truth about his Son. What should we do now?" As the men talked and prayed, they immediately grasped their new mission for Jesus: to spread the news of his birth swiftly. As they hastened through Bethlehem, they eagerly shared their miraculous experience with everyone they encountered.

Luke tells us of the shepherds' mission: "*And when they had seen it, they made known abroad the saying which was told them concerning this child. And all they that heard it wondered at those things which were told them by the shepherds*" (Luke 2:17–18).

After meeting Jesus, the shepherds' hearts were ablaze. Their hope was a radiant beacon inside them, and they were eager to share what they had seen and heard. It was impossible to contain their excitement. As they strolled through Bethlehem, they shared the wonderful news with everyone they met, their faith, joy, and hope shining through every word.

"We saw angels!" they said. "They told us about a special baby in a stable. We found him just like they said we would! He's the One God promised to send. He's here to bring salvation and hope to everyone!"

A young boy tugged at his mother's sleeve. "Mama, can we go see the baby?" he asked, his eyes wide with wonder after hearing the shepherds' tale.

A shepherd knelt, smiling. "He's in a stable, little one. The King of kings, born among the animals."

The shepherds became fervent messengers of hope, seizing every opportunity to share their incredible story. With each new encounter, they eagerly retold the angelic visitation, the heavenly choir, and the miracle of finding the baby Jesus as foretold. Their voices rang out passionately!

The innkeeper, who had turned away Mary and Joseph, listened intently. "A baby, you say? In one of the stables?" He scratched his head, realization dawning. "I had no idea . . . "

The once-gruff shepherds were transformed, their eyes sparkling and voices ringing with joy as they celebrated the beautiful things they had witnessed. Their stories spread quickly, like a tiny flame catching dry leaves. Their transformation from ordinary shepherds to devoted messengers of hope was inspiring.

People in town stopped to listen to their excited stories about that fantastic night. Before long, the talk of the town was about the baby Jesus being born in a stable. Everyone was amazed that God had picked simple shepherds to share such big news.

As they entered the marketplace, a cloth merchant eyed them suspiciously. "Angels, you say? In the fields?" He scoffed. But as the shepherds described the heavenly choir, the merchant's expression softened, and he leaned in to hear more.

The town's rabbi listened intently, stroking his beard. "A Savior, born in Bethlehem?" he mused. "Just as the prophet Micah foretold. Perhaps ... perhaps it's time to visit this child myself."

A small caravan of travelers stopped for supplies and gathered around the shepherds. "We must spread this news in our homeland," one said excitedly. "The Messiah has come!"

Luke continues with their mission: *"And the shepherds returned, glorifying and praising God for all the things that they had heard and seen, as it was told unto them"* (Luke 2:20).

A Roman soldier on patrol overheard the commotion. "What's all this about a new king?" he demanded gruffly. Undaunted, the shepherds shared their story, watching as the soldier's stern face gave way to thoughtful curiosity.

An older woman bent with age, grasped a shepherd's arm. "I've waited all my life for this news," she whispered, tears in her eyes. "Tell me more about this Savior."

As you can see, not everyone reacted the same way to this Good News. But Luke tells us that everyone wondered about the shepherd's words. Some people were amazed, while others just questioned. Each person felt something different in their heart. But even if some were skeptical about the Messiah's coming, the shepherds kept sharing what they had heard and seen. They were so sure about what they had experienced that they didn't give up, no matter what others thought.

When people doubt or question God's truth, we can learn from these shepherds. Their example shows us how to faithfully and courageously proclaim the Good News of Jesus. As believers in Christ, we should follow their example. We, too, should share the message of the hope, joy, and salvation Jesus brings. This is the true message of Christmas, one we can share all year.

"Go tell it on the mountain,
over the hills, and ev'rywhere;
go, tell it on the mountain
that Jesus Christ is born."[27]

---

27 "Go, Tell It on the Mountain," by John W. Work, the first verse of an African American spiritual. Public domain.

CHAPTER 9

THE PONDERING—LUKE 2:19 (WEDNESDAY)

The night was peaceful. Mary held her newborn baby boy, Jesus, in her arms. While everyone else was asleep, Mary had a quiet moment to think about all the amazing things that had happened. She looked at his tiny face, certain this child would shape the future in ways yet unknown. The Bible describes it this way: "*But Mary kept all these things and pondered them in her heart*" (Luke 2:19).

These words help us see inside Mary's mind. She was thinking about all the beautiful things God had done. She was amazed by the angels and shepherds who had come to see Jesus. Mary knew these events were of vital importance, so she kept these precious memories in her heart.

It all began when the angel visited her with a surprising but comforting message. Mary thought about how Jesus came to be in a way no other baby ever had. God had made her pregnant in a manner no one could explain. Then, the Roman rulers made a law that brought her and Joseph to this simple stable. She remembered each detail of all these incredible events.

Mary was just a simple girl from Nazareth, but God had chosen her to be the mother of his only begotten Son. On this quiet night, she realized how important this gift from God was. She knew God didn't choose her because she was special or better than others but because of his grace, kindness, and love. This filled Mary with amazement and gratitude for God's goodness toward her.

Baby Jesus moved in Mary's arms, causing her to remember the extraordinary things people had said about him. She remembered what the angel Gabriel had told her—that her baby was the Promised One, the long-awaited Messiah. Mary felt both valuable to God and insignificant at the same time. She was amazed that God, so big and powerful, had become this tiny, helpless baby.

In the soft light of the stable, Mary accepted her extraordinary job as Jesus's mother. As she held her newborn son, she realized this was just the beginning of an incredible journey. Her mind drifted from the present moment to the years ahead. She thought about how amazing it was to be part of God's plan for the world and began to wonder about Jesus's future. What would her son do when he grew up? What great things did God have planned for him?

When the Bible says, "Mary kept all these things," it means that she did more than vaguely remember what happened. She carefully thought about every little detail. Mary stored all these memories like precious treasures: the stable, Jesus's birth, the bright star, and the shepherds who came to visit Jesus. She knew they were all part of the story of God's plan of salvation.

As Mary sat quietly in the night, she felt thankful, humble, and amazed. Everything that had happened in the past few months was miraculous. She could see how God had planned it all. In the quiet, Mary whispered, "Thank you," to her heavenly Father. God had chosen her to be a valued part of his plan to save the world through Jesus, the Christ, her Son.

As we journey through this Advent season, Mary's thoughtful pondering offers us a beautiful example. Like her, we can pause and reflect on the amazing things God has done in our lives. We're invited to treasure the gift of Jesus in our hearts, just as Mary did. This season of waiting and hope reminds us to look forward with excitement to all that God will do through Jesus. As we prepare to celebrate his birth, let's follow Mary's lead—pondering God's love, embracing the hope Jesus brings, and anticipating the beautiful ways he'll work in our lives. In these quiet moments of reflection, we, too, can find ourselves part of God's incredible story of salvation.

"Why lies He in such mean estate
Where ox and lamb are feeding?
Good Christian, fear, for sinners here
The silent Word is pleading.
Nails, spear shall pierce Him through
The cross be borne for me, for you
Hail, hail the Word made flesh
The Babe, the Son of Mary."[28]

---

28 William C. Dix, "What Child Is This," Sovereign Grace Music, Dayspring Music LLC, 1865.

CHAPTER 10

THE NAME—LUKE 2:21 (THURSDAY)

The sun peeked over the hills of Judea, painting Bethlehem in warm, golden light. The little town woke up, buzzing with whispers of a story that would be told forever. It had been a week since baby Jesus was born. Finding a simple home in Bethlehem to stay in, Joseph and Mary watched the tiny baby who would bring salvation to the world. This young family loved and obeyed God more than anything.

Jesus was now eight days old. In Jewish tradition, the eighth day was special. God told Abraham long ago that baby boys should be circumcised on this day. Circumcision was a special ceremony where a small piece of skin was removed from a baby boy. It was a way to show that the child belonged to Abraham's family. This tradition had been followed for thousands of years.

Mary and Joseph remembered God's Law: "And on the eighth day, the flesh of his foreskin shall be circumcised" (Leviticus 12:3).

Baby Jesus was unique, unlike any other child.[29] King David once said about himself, "Behold, I was [shaped] in iniquity; And in sin did my mother conceive me" (Psalm 51:5). David knew that he was a sinner.[30] But Jesus was different. He was born without sin because God's Holy Spirit was

---

29 Jesus is fully God, and fully man, and was called, "The Son of God," and "The Son of Man."

30 David was not saying that his parents conceiving him was evil. Through these words in Psalm 51:5, he recognized his inherent moral weakness. He acknowledged that he possessed a sinful nature. This implies that throughout his entire life, there was never a point at which he was completely free from sin or the inclination toward it. His dilemma is the same for each of us.

his Father.[31] Jesus was so good that he didn't need rules to tell him how to live right. He was even above the Law. But here's the amazing thing: even though he was perfect, Jesus chose to follow all the rules. By doing this, he showed he was human like us. Jesus wanted to identify with sinners, even though he never did anything wrong himself.

The day had arrived. Luke tells us about this critical moment: *"And when eight days were accomplished for the circumcising of the child, his name was called JESUS, which was so named of the angel before he was conceived in the womb"* (Luke 2:21).

Mary and Joseph loved God deeply and obediently took their tiny son to follow the old Hebrew tradition. This act unfolded as a solemn covenant, a binding promise. By this painful ceremony, God's Son followed all of God's Law. The Bible says, "Every man that is circumcised . . . is a debtor to do the whole Law" (Galatians 5:3). After Adam and Eve disobeyed God, no one could follow all of God's rules perfectly—until Jesus Christ came. This holy child, the Son of Man, would obey God's rules his whole life. This way, he could be the perfect sacrifice to take away our sins!

Jesus's obedience to the Law was crucial to being our Savior. By following every rule perfectly, he did what no one else could, making him the only one who could take our punishment. Because he never sinned, Jesus could offer himself as a perfect sacrifice for us. His obedience didn't just show he was good—it was a key part of God's plan to save us. Because Jesus followed the Law, he paved the way for our forgiveness and freedom.

The Bible tells us that Jesus was "made of a woman, made under the Law" for a special reason—to save us. He came "to redeem them that were under the law, that we might receive the adoption[32] of sons" (Galatians 4:5). When baby Jesus was circumcised, he promised to follow God's rules. By doing this, he "[*has*] redeemed us from the curse of the Law." How? Later,

---

31 This is why the Virgin Birth was necessary for him.

32 The believer's salvation is seen as both "the New Birth" into God's family (the Apostle John), and as being "adopted" into God's family (the Apostle Paul).

at his crucifixion on Mount Calvary, he will take our sins on himself,[33] "being made a curse[34] for us" (Galatians 3:13). Jesus obeyed his Father. He was "obedient unto death, even the death of the cross" (Philippians 2:8).

Isn't this amazing? Jesus, who never sinned, chose to die for us. He took the punishment we deserved. When he died on the cross, he carried all our sins. He paid the price to make things right between God and us. This is why the angel told Mary and Joseph to name their baby "Jesus." In Jewish tradition, giving a name during the circumcision ceremony was very important. The name "Jesus" means "Savior" (Matthew 1:21; Acts 13:23). And that's precisely what Jesus is: the Savior that God sent to find us when we're lost in our sin and bring us back to him. Jesus is the only one who can do this for us.

These beautiful truths show us Jesus, who, by obeying God, made a way for us to be saved. His Name brings hope, kindness, and never-ending love to all God's children. This is who the Christmas baby is—Jesus, "the Savior."

"I know of a Name,
A beautiful Name,
That unto a Babe was given;
The stars glittered bright
Throughout that glad night,
And angels praised God in heaven.
That beautiful Name, that beautiful Name,
From sin has power to free us!
That beautiful Name, that wonderful Name,
That matchless Name is Jesus!"[35]

---

33 On the cross when he is crucified, Jesus will take on himself all sin, for every person, for all time. There he will pay the sin debt for the world all at one time.

34 The Bible says (Deuteronomy 21:22–23) that "for he that is hanged is accursed of God." When Jesus hung on "Calvary's tree" for your sin and mine, he was cursed by his Father!

35 "That Beautiful Name," by Jean Perry. The second verse and refrain. Public domain.

CHAPTER 11

THE SACRIFICE—LUKE 2:22-24 (FRIDAY)

Following Jesus's birth, Mary's heart was filled with a mother's love and a desire to obey God. As a new mother, she prepared to bring Jesus to the Temple and offer sacrifices, just as God's Law required. Luke tells us about this particular moment:

> *And when the days of her purification according to the law of Moses were accomplished, they brought Him [Jesus] to Jerusalem, to present Him to the Lord; (As it is written in the law of the Lord, "Every male that openeth the womb shall be called holy to the Lord;") And to offer a sacrifice according to that which is said in the Law of the Lord, "A pair of turtledoves, or two young pigeons." (Luke 2:22–24)*

Back in those days, new mothers had a special forty-day time of rest after having a baby boy. During this time, they stayed home and didn't visit the Temple. When the forty days were over, they would take their baby boy to the Temple. There, they would show him to God, give thanks for his birth, and ask for God's blessing on the child. The new mom would also give a sacrifice to God, usually two birds. This all happened right after their waiting time ended. Mary loved and trusted God. She joyfully obeyed him.

Being kind and humble, Mary got ready to do what God's Law asked of her. She carefully followed the old rules (Leviticus 12:2–3) that Moses had taught. These rules (Leviticus 12:6) said a mother should bring two gifts to God: a lamb and a bird, or just two birds if the family didn't have much money. Since Mary and Joseph weren't rich, and were far from home in Bethlehem, Mary offered two birds.

Mary's gifts showed her love for God and her desire to follow him. By giving these gifts, she told God, "I'm sorry for my sins, and I want to live for you." These gifts were important because they helped her become "clean" in God's eyes after having a baby, allowing her to worship in the Temple again.

Throughout her life, Mary showed how much she loved and trusted God. She knew she wasn't perfect. In her beautiful prayer, she said, "I praise the Lord with all my heart. I am very happy because God is my Savior" (Luke 1: 46–47 ERV). By calling God her Savior, Mary showed that she, like everyone else, needed God's forgiveness. The Bible tells us, "For all have sinned and come short of the glory of God" (Romans 3:23). Mary humbly understood that this truth included her too.

Jesus, Mary's Son, was different from his mother and all of us. He never did anything wrong, so he never needed to ask for forgiveness or present a sin offering. That's why Jesus is called the spotless Lamb of God—he is perfect and pure.

On the fortieth day after Jesus's birth, Mary was ready with her gifts. The gentle sounds of cooing birds filled the air as she entered the Temple that day. With love and care, she brought her baby to present him to the Lord in this holy place. Every step she took showed her obedience, and every beat of her heart sang of her love for God. As she stood there, Mary must have felt both humble and thankful. She was doing what God asked, even though she didn't fully understand his plan. She happily did her part.

Mary's obedience in offering her sacrifice and presenting Jesus at the Temple set the stage for God's greater plan. Her humble act of faith pointed to the ultimate sacrifice her Son would make. Just as Mary brought her offering to God, Jesus would one day offer himself for humanity. This story of obedience, sacrifice, and hope continues to challenge and inspire us today.

As we reflect on Mary's faithfulness and the promise of hope for salvation through Jesus Christ, we're reminded of the words from the beloved hymn "We Three Kings." Though often associated with the Magi, this verse beautifully captures the essence of Jesus's mission, foreshadowed by Mary's obedient act in the Temple. These lyrics echo the themes of our chapter—Jesus as King, God, and Sacrifice. They remind us that the baby Mary presented in the Temple, God in the flesh, would become our perfect sacrifice, leading us to God's love and the forgiveness of our sins:

"Glorious now behold Him arise;
King and God and Sacrifice:
Alleluia, Alleluia,
sounds through the earth and skies.
O star of wonder, star of light,
star with royal beauty bright,
westward leading, still proceeding,
guide us to thy perfect light."[36]

---

36 We Three Kings of Orient Are," by John H. Hopkins (1857), the fifth verse and refrain. Public domain.

CHAPTER 12

THE WATCHER—LUKE 2:25-27 (SATURDAY)

An older man named Simeon lived in a quiet part of Jerusalem among ancient city walls. He walked slowly, supported by a cane. Though his eyes were getting weaker, they shone with bright hope. His wrinkled face was evidence that he had lived many years. As the sun went down, turning the sky orange and purple, Simeon stood in the Temple again, patiently waiting. Simeon's life was filled with hope as he waited for God's promise to come true.

The Bible tells us about this faithful man:

And, behold, there was a man in Jerusalem, whose name was Simeon; and the same man was just and devout, waiting for the consolation of Israel[37]: and the Holy Ghost[38] was upon him. And it was revealed unto him by the Holy Ghost, that he should not see death before he had seen the Lord's Christ. And he came by the Spirit into the Temple: and when the parents brought in the child Jesus, to do for Him after the custom of the law. (Luke 2:25–27)

---

37 "The Consolation of Israel" refers to the Jewish people's hope and expectation for the coming of the Messiah. This Messiah was expected to bring Israel comfort, redemption, and restoration. This "consolation" is fulfilled in the person of Jesus Christ.

38 "Holy Ghost" was the old Middle English way of saying "Holy Spirit." Over time, as the English language evolved, and "ghost" took on more specific connotations related to the spirits of the dead, later translations and revisions of the Bible shifted toward using "Holy Spirit" to avoid confusion and more accurately reflect the original meaning. It's worth noting that there is no theological difference between "Holy Ghost" and "Holy Spirit"—they refer to the same concept in Christian theology. The change in terminology is purely linguistic.

Of all the men named Simeon in Jerusalem, Luke only tells us about one. This Simeon was exceptional. The Bible calls him a "good and devoted man." This means he had a close relationship with God, followed his Word, and gave his whole life in service to him. Simeon had a good heart and good actions, which caused other people who loved God to look up to him.

Because Simeon was a righteous man, he felt a deep longing in his heart. He was waiting for something special—for God to comfort Israel.[39] Luke's words show us what was most important to Simeon: his heart held tight to God's promises. Even when times were hard, Simeon's hope in God's promise kept him going. He genuinely wanted to see the day the Messiah would come. This Messiah would bring comfort and save God's people.

Simeon had been waiting for "the consolation of Israel." This meant he hoped God would send the promised Messiah, who would rescue and comfort the Jewish people. This hope wasn't new. It started long ago in Bible times. Early leaders like Jacob talked about it (Genesis 49:18), and later, prophets like Isaiah wrote about it (Isaiah 40:1).

So people who loved God kept waiting—for a very long time. Simeon, like many others, carried this old hope with him. He remembered the promises about a Savior who would come to make things right and save people.

Think about how long Simeon waited—the years stretched like a giant desert. Every day, he longed for God to fulfill his Word. He saw his people go through good times and bad, knowing everyone wanted to see the Messiah. Through it all, Simeon never gave up believing God's promise.

The Temple was a special place where people prayed and gave offerings to God. For Simeon, it became his favorite place to live out his strong faith. He would stand in the Temple's open areas, breathing in the sweet smell of incense the priests used. He carefully watched everyone who came in, hoping to spot the Messiah, "the Lord's Christ."[40] In his mind, he

---

39 The "Consolation of Israel."
40 These are more names for Jesus.

sang the psalms David wrote long ago. He talked to God as if talking to a close friend.

Mary and Joseph brought baby Jesus to the Temple because this was the Jewish custom that parents followed with their firstborn sons. They came to dedicate Jesus to God and to offer Mary's sacrifices, following the rules God gave in the Bible.

On a day God chose, Simeon's long wait finally ended. Led by God's Spirit to the Temple, Simeon held the Christ child in his arms. This baby was the hope Simeon had been waiting for—God's promise made real. Immediately, he knew this was the Messiah and said, "Lord, I can die in peace now. I've seen the Savior you promised" (Luke 2:29–30, paraphrased).

God let Simeon, who had waited so faithfully, not just see but also hold the promise he'd believed in for so long. The comfort he'd been waiting for was in his arms. Simeon must have felt overjoyed. His hope had finally become real.

Simeon's story shows us how important it is to trust God, patiently watching and waiting for his promises to be fulfilled. We can trust that at the right time, God will make his promises come true in ways we can see and feel, just like he did for Simeon. Everyone who obeys God and faithfully waits for him will find lasting comfort when Jesus returns. Like Simeon, we can have hope in God's promises, even when we must wait. As we'll see next week, there's even more we can learn from Simeon's profound encounter with the Christ child.

"O come, O come, Immanuel,
and ransom captive Israel
that mourns in lonely exile here
until the Son of God appear.
Rejoice! Rejoice! Immanuel
shall come to you, O Israel."[41]

---

41 "O Come, O Come, Emmanuel," From the 12th century Latin. Translator: J. M. Neale (1851). The first verse and refrain. Public domain.

THIRD WEEK SCRIPTURE READING (SUNDAY)

Then took he him up in his arms, and blessed God, and said,

"Lord, now lettest thou thy servant depart

In peace, according to thy word:

For mine eyes have seen thy salvation,

Which thou hast prepared before the face of all people;

A light to lighten the Gentiles, and the glory of thy people Israel."

And Joseph and his mother marvelled at those things which were spoken of him. And Simeon blessed them, and said unto Mary his mother, "Behold, this child is set for the fall and rising again of many in Israel; and for a sign which shall be spoken against; (Yea, a sword shall pierce through thy own soul also,) that the thoughts of many hearts may be revealed."

And there was one Anna, a prophetess, the daughter of Phanuel, of the tribe of Aser: she was of a great age, and had lived with an husband seven years from her virginity; And she was a widow of about fourscore and four years, which departed not from the temple, but served God with fastings and prayers night and day. And she coming in that instant gave thanks likewise unto the Lord, and spake of him to all them that looked for redemption in Jerusalem.

And when they had performed all things according to the law of the Lord, they returned into Galilee, to their own city Nazareth. And the child grew, and waxed strong in spirit, filled with wisdom: and the grace of God was upon him.

—Luke 2:28–40

CHAPTER 13

THE PROPHECY—LUKE 2:28–32 (MONDAY)

As Simeon held baby Jesus in his arms, he was overwhelmed with joy and gratitude. He knew God had fulfilled his divine promise. Simeon started to pray, and his words were powerful. In the Christmas story, we can read what Simeon said:

> *Then took he Him up in his arms, and blessed God, and said, "Lord, now [let] thou thy servant depart in peace, according to thy Word: For mine eyes have seen Thy Salvation, Which thou hast prepared before the face of all people; A light to lighten the Gentiles,*[42] *and the glory of thy people Israel."* (Luke 2:28–32)

What did Simeon mean by these words? They show the peace he felt because God had done what he said he would do. Simeon had been waiting long to see the Messiah, and now his heart was happy because God had brought his promise to him. When Simeon said, "I have seen your salvation!" he was talking about Jesus.

Simeon recognized Jesus as the promised Savior. His words show that Jesus came for everyone, all sinners—not just one group but all the people of the world. No matter who or where you're from, Jesus came for you. In ancient times, only the Jewish people knew about Jehovah God because of what Moses and the prophets taught them. But by *Gentiles*, Simeon was referring to all who were not members of the Jewish people. Simeon

---

42 The non-Jewish peoples.

acknowledged that Jesus would help everyone learn about God and how to have a personal relationship with him.

We call Jesus our Savior, just like we call him our Hope, Peace, and Life. For everyone who believes in Jesus and trusts him to save them, he is all these things and much more!

Simeon also said that Jesus would "bring honor to your people, Israel." This means that Jesus was the Messiah, the person God had promised to send to the Jewish people. God had made an everlasting commitment, called a covenant, to Abraham and his descendants, who became the Jewish nation. Jesus was the One who made all of God's promises to them come true.

Simeon's hope wasn't just for himself. It was a hope for all people, a hope that continues today. Jesus brings us hope that our sins can be forgiven, hope that we can know God personally, and hope for a better future. This hope isn't an idle wish—it's a sure promise from God, just like he gave to Simeon. Jesus, the Son of God, is the light that shows all people the truth about God. In him, those lost in spiritual darkness can now find their way to God.

Jesus doesn't just offer hope—he *is* Hope. For everyone who believes in him, Jesus is our Savior, Peace, and Life. If we turn away from our sins and trust in him, he changes us from the inside out. He brings us close to God. He gives us a new life and a fresh start.

Jesus isn't just a historical figure or a good teacher from long ago. He's alive and active today! He is God's Living Word.[43] God's Holy Spirit helps us understand the Bible. When we read it, God speaks to us directly, helping us to know Jesus better and apply his teachings to our lives.

Ultimately, Simeon's prophecy wasn't just about a baby in a temple. It was about God's incredible love reaching out to every person, offering life and a personal relationship with the Creator of the universe. That's the

---

43 As the Living Word, Jesus helps us understand God's message in a way that makes sense to us today, and he puts that message into action in our lives.

power and promise of Jesus—he is the Light that never dims, the Hope that never fades, and the Love that never ends.

Jesus is reaching out to you today. What about you? Do you know him? Is he your Savior? Have you asked him to forgive your sins and cleanse your heart? You can talk to Jesus right now. If you turn to him by faith, you can ask him to save you: "Behold, now is the accepted time; behold, now is the day of salvation" (2 Corinthians 6:2b).

"Led by the light of faith serenely beaming,
With glowing hearts by His cradle we stand.
So led by light of a star sweetly gleaming,
Here came the Wise Men from Orient land.
The King of kings lay thus in lowly manger,
In all our trials born to be our Friend.
He knows our need—to our weakness is no stranger.
Behold your King, before Him lowly bend!
Behold your King, before Him lowly bend!"[44]

---

44 "O Holy Night," by Placide Cappeau (1847, French). Translator, John S. Dwight. Second verse. Public domain.

CHAPTER 14

THE PROMISE—LUKE 2:33–35 (TUESDAY)

Mary and Joseph listened intently as Simeon began to speak about the baby's future. His words were so powerful that Mary and Joseph were in awe. In the Bible, Luke tells us what Simeon said:

And Joseph and his mother marveled at those things which were spoken of him. And Simeon blessed them and said unto Mary, his mother, "Behold, this child is set for the fall and rising again of many in Israel and for a sign which shall be spoken against. Yea, a sword shall pierce through thy own soul also, that the thoughts of many hearts may be revealed." (Luke 2:33–35)

Mary and Joseph were surprised by Simeon's words. Jesus was just a tiny baby, but Simeon spoke of him as if he held the world's future in his little hands. Simeon's words painted a picture of a grown-up Jesus who would reshape the course of history.

Imagine how Mary and Joseph felt. They were still learning about their special baby. But here was Simeon, someone they'd just met, saying all these incredible things about him. Simeon knew things about Jesus that even his parents didn't know yet! His words were wise and full of promise, but they also contained a warning.

Simeon said Jesus would make some people "fall" and others "rise." This meant he would make people choose to be for or against him. Those who follow Jesus "rise"—they get closer to God. Those who don't follow him "fall"—sadly, they move further away from God.

We can see this happening when Jesus grew up and began his ministry. Jesus's words and actions made people choose whether or not to follow him. Here are two examples from the Bible that show how different people responded:

A wealthy young man walked away from Jesus sad because he loved his money too much.[45] He "fell" by choosing his wealth over Jesus.

But others welcomed Jesus's teachings:

Zacchaeus, who used to cheat people, changed completely.[46] He "rose" by following Jesus and making things right with everyone he had wronged.

These two Bible characters show us how Jesus's presence forced people to choose, just like Simeon said it would.

Even today, everyone must decide what they will do with Jesus—no one can remain neutral. When people hear about Jesus, they must carefully consider whether to accept or reject him—whether they will "rise" or "fall."

This reminds us of a moment of choice from the Bible. God had saved the Israelites from bondage in Egypt. Then, through their leader, Moses, he gave them rules. These rules (God's Law) showed them how to live in a way that pleased God, their Deliverer.

Before Moses died, he told the people they had to make a serious choice. He said: "I call heaven and earth to record this day against you, that I have set before you life and death, blessing and cursing: therefore choose life, that both thou and thy seed may live" (Deuteronomy 30:19).

In simpler words, Moses was saying, "Pay attention! This is vitally important. God is giving you two choices: you can choose to follow him and live a life of blessing, or you can choose to disobey him, which leads to trouble, sadness, and destruction (*rise or fall*). I'm telling you to follow God so that you and your children can please him!"

---

45 Jesus's teaching about the "Rich Young Ruler" can be found in Matthew 19:16–30, Mark 10:17–27, and Luke 18:18–27.

46 Jesus's interaction with Zaccheus is found in Luke 19:1–10.

Many years later, Simeon said baby Jesus would grow up and ask people to make a choice, too, just like the Israelites. This choice is paramount. It's about choosing between living forever with God in heaven or being separated from him forever in hell. That's why what you choose to do with Jesus is critical.

Simeon also warned that many people would speak against Jesus. This part of his prophecy came true too. Here's what it means: Jesus came to our world with a message of hope. He showed us God's truth and offered a way to fix the problems caused by sin. Following Jesus leads to a bright future. But not everyone liked what Jesus said or did.

Imagine a world full of darkness, and Jesus comes as a bright light. Some people run to the light, happy to see clearly. Others, though, turn away or try to argue that the darkness is better. They don't want to change or admit they need help.

So just as Simeon said, many people argue against Jesus and his teachings. They choose to stay in the darkness of sin rather than accept the hope and new life Jesus offers. We all face this choice: Will we welcome Jesus's light and hope or turn away from it?

Simeon also had a special message for Mary. He wanted her to know that being Jesus's mother would bring heartache. He said, "A sword shall pierce through thy own soul also." This meant Mary would feel much pain, especially when people rejected Jesus and when he died on the cross. God's warning through Simeon gave Mary hope for the difficult times ahead. She could face them with the knowledge that God is in control.

Simeon concluded his words to Mary: "that the thoughts of many hearts may be revealed." What is revealed when the light of Jesus shines on your heart and mind?

Jesus invites you to let him cleanse your heart. He offers forgiveness for your sins.

Today, will you step into the sunshine instead of staying in the shadows? He's waiting with open arms, ready to give you a fresh start and a heart full of hope.

"Hail the heaven-born Prince of Peace!
Hail the Sun of Righteousness!
Light and life to all he brings,
risen with healing in his wings.
Mild he lays his glory by,
born that man no more may die,
born to raise us from the earth,
born to give us second birth.
Hark! the herald angels sing,
'Glory to the newborn King!'"[47]

---

47 "Hark! the Herald Angels Sing," by Charles Wesley (1739), third verse and refrain. Alterer: George Whitefield. Public domain.

CHAPTER 15

THE SERVANT—LUKE 2:36– 37 (WEDNESDAY)

Anna was a faithful servant of God whose life is part of the Christmas story. People have told her story for a long time because she shows us what it means to be truly devoted to God. God had a special plan for Anna's life.

Every day, Anna would wake up before sunrise. As she made her way through the Temple, she'd take a deep breath, smiling at the familiar scent of olive-oil lamps and the soft glow of their light. Despite her age, she moved quickly through the Temple, eager to share her message. Even though she had faced many difficult challenges, she never stopped trusting God. By the end of her long life, Anna had become an example of strong faith and dedication to God.

We learn about Anna in the Bible. Luke writes:

And there was one Anna, a prophetess, the daughter of Phanuel, of the tribe of Aser: she was of a great age, and had lived with an husband seven years from her virginity; And she was a widow of about fourscore and four years, which departed not from the temple, but served God with fastings and prayers night and day." (Luke 2:36–37)

Anna came from a family with deep roots in the tribe of Asher,[48] one of God's chosen people's twelve tribes. As a young woman, Anna married and looked forward to a long life with her husband, but she was widowed at a young age. Many people might have become bitter after such a loss, but not Anna. In her grief, she turned to God for comfort, purpose, and hope.

The Temple in Jerusalem became her home. Day after day, year after year, Anna could be found there, praying and fasting. As Anna grew older, her love for God grew stronger. While others slept, Anna prayed. When others ate, she often fasted, focusing all her energy on talking to God.

People in Jerusalem began to recognize Anna as a prophetess who shared messages from God. Being a prophetess, Anna was close to God. She spoke his truth to others. Everyone who met her could tell from her demeanor and character that she was a woman who spent much time in God's presence. Through the years, her hair grayed, and her steps slowed, but Anna's devotion grew. For more than eighty years, Anna lived this way. Her life was not easy, but she found joy in serving God. Through good times and bad, Anna loved her Lord. And her life became a living example of how powerful God's love can be.

The story of Anna's devotion isn't just a part of Bible history—it speaks directly to our lives today. She shows us how to stay focused on God in a world of distractions. Anna spent her days praying, fasting, and helping others. By doing this, she found real happiness and purpose in her life.

We can follow Anna's example. We can pray to God, and our prayers can be like a sweet smell to him. Then, we can show our love for him by

---

48 "Aser" is the name of the tribe as written in New Testament Greek. "Asher" is the same name from Old Testament Hebrew. The bulk of the Old Testament was originally penned in Hebrew, and the New Testament in Koiné Greek. Teaching about the Twelve Tribes of Israel is found in the Old Testament. In modern biblical scholarship and general usage, "Asher" is the preferred spelling when referring to this Israelite tribe. In the book of Genesis, the origins of the tribes are traced to the sons of Jacob (later renamed Israel). Genesis chapters 29 through 30 describe the births of Jacob's sons. Genesis chapter 49 contains Jacob's blessings and prophecies for each of his sons, which became associated with their respective tribes.

helping others. With our hearts focused on him, our service to others will be done in the right spirit. Our motivation will not be "the praise of men" (John 12:43) but to glorify our heavenly Father. We can use King David's prayer to help us: "Create in me a clean heart, O God; And renew a right spirit within me" (Psalm 51:10).

While waiting for Jesus to return, we remember Anna's example. Her resilience shines like a bright light, guiding us through the twists and turns of life. May we remain as devoted as Anna was as we age, and the fruit of our lives be sweet as we serve God with all our hearts. When Jesus returns, may he find us faithfully waiting, watching, and serving!

But Anna's story doesn't end there. All those years of praying and serving led to something extraordinary—something Anna had been waiting for her whole life. As Anna went about her daily routine in the Temple, she had no idea this day would be different. All her years of waiting and working had brought her to this moment. She was about to meet a miracle that would set God's plan of redemption in motion. Who was this *miracle* Anna was about to meet? Anna's unwavering faith foreshadowed *The Dawn of Hope* that she was about to meet in the person of Jesus Christ.

"O come, all ye faithful, Joyful and triumphant,
O come ye, O come ye to Bethlehem.
Come and behold Him, born the King of angels;
O come, let us adore Him,
O come, let us adore Him,
O come, let us adore Him, Christ the Lord!"[49]

---

49 "O Come, All Ye Faithful," attributed to John Francis Wade. Translator: Frederick Oakley (1841). The first verse and refrain. Public domain.

CHAPTER 16

THE PROCLAIMER—LUKE 2:38 (THURSDAY)

The Temple in Jerusalem was a grand building with tall stone walls and shining gold decorations. Its huge doors opened to reveal a bustling courtyard filled with people. The air smelled of incense and echoed with prayers and quiet conversations. Anna loved being here, but she loved God more. For over eighty years, Anna served God in this place, holding onto hope that she would see God's promise fulfilled. Her hope never wavered, even as she grew old. Her faith was massive, and today, it would meet a miracle.

The Temple was always busy, but this day had an extra buzz of excitement. People whispered to each other, their faces full of hope and wonder. Something extraordinary was about to happen, and Anna sensed it.

Anna found them just as Simeon was finishing talking with Joseph and Mary about Jesus. Her face lit up like a bright star when she saw the child. She saw hope in human form. Her old eyes filled with happy tears, and her hands trembled excitedly. She realized all her years of waiting and hoping for the Messiah had led to this moment. She knew Jesus was the One God promised and felt overwhelmed with gratitude. The Bible says: *"And she coming in that instant gave thanks . . . unto the Lord, and [spoke] of Him to all them that looked for redemption in Jerusalem"* (Luke 2:38).[50]

---

50 This phrase, "looking for redemption in Jerusalem," is like the phrase "waiting for the consolation of Israel" (Luke 2:25).

Anna was a prophetess who sought the Messiah God had promised. Upon meeting the Christ child, her heart echoed the words of Zechariah, John the Baptist's father. He said, "Blessed *be* the Lord God of Israel, For He hath *visited* and *redeemed* His people" (Luke 1:68).

Zechariah's words were full of hope. He knew that Jesus's birth meant God was keeping his promise to save his people. He tells us two key things about Jesus. The first is that God came to be with us. Jesus is God who became a human to live with us and die for us. The second is that Jesus came to save us. The Bible says this is "redemption." It means that Jesus came to free us from our sins, forgive us, and bring us back to God. The Bible calls Jesus the "Lamb of God" and says he came to "redeem us." He is the God-man who is the only One who can free us from our sins.

This is of great importance because it means Jesus is the only Savior. The Bible tells us there's no other way to come to God except through Jesus (Acts 4:10–12). Anna was so excited to tell everyone about him!

Anna spoke to all kinds of people in the Temple—young mothers with babies on their hips, bearded older men leaning on walking sticks, curious children with wide eyes, and busy merchants taking breaks from their work. They all stopped to listen when Anna began to speak about the special baby.

People trusted Anna when she talked about Jesus. She was so happy in her faith that she told everyone who would listen about him. Luke wrote about Anna and said she "spoke about Him (the child)."[51] This means Anna was more than just telling a story. She was sharing the Good News that the One who brought hope and could change people's lives was born and living right here with them! She couldn't keep the Good News to herself. Anna shared it with everyone she met in the Temple.

---

51 Anna told them that Jesus was the One they had been waiting for. He is the *Redeemer* and the *Consolation of Israel*. These two thoughts will be completely fulfilled at his second Advent.

Just like Anna found hope in Jesus, we, too, can find hope in him today. Jesus offers us the same hope he brought to Anna. And just like her, we can share the joy of that hope with others.

Let's think about how we can follow Anna's example in our own lives:

1. **Be thankful every day.** Anna spent years serving God in the Temple, always grateful for his promises. We, too, can find many reasons to thank God daily, no matter what's happening in our lives.

2. **Look for Jesus.** Anna recognized Jesus as the promised Savior. We can faithfully wait and watch for Jesus's return. When Jesus returned to heaven, the angels promised his disciples, "This same Jesus, which is taken up from you into heaven, shall so come in like manner as ye have seen Him go into heaven" (Acts 1:11).

3. **Share the Good News.** Anna told everyone about Jesus. We can do the same by talking with our friends, family, and people we meet about what Jesus means to us. When we share Jesus, we're not just telling a story—we're offering hope to others. Anna's hope led her to tell everyone about Jesus. Our hope can do the same for us.

Here's a challenge for you: Let's be like Anna this Christmas. Let's purpose in our hearts to thank God every day for what he's done and share Jesus's love with someone.

Telling others about Jesus might feel scary, but remember:

- Jesus's story is the most important message ever!
- Everyone needs the hope Jesus brings.
- Start small and take baby steps as you learn to share.
- Think of how excited Anna was—you can be excited too; you are sharing the truth!

Will you take this challenge? Can you be a messenger of hope this week? Anna shows us that hope in Jesus is worth waiting for and sharing.

"We've a message to give to the nations,
that the Lord who reigneth above
has sent us His Son to save us,
and show us that God is love,
and show us that God is love.

"We've a Savior to show to the nations,
who the path of sorrow has trod,
that all of the world's great peoples
may come to the truth of God,
may come to the truth of God!

"For the darkness shall turn to dawning,
and the dawning to noonday bright,
and Christ's great kingdom shall come [to] earth,
the kingdom of love and light."[52]

---

52 "We've a Story to Tell to the Nations," by H. Ernest Nichol, 1896. Copyright status:
public domain. These are the third and fourth verses with the refrain.

CHAPTER 17

THE FAMILY—LUKE 2:39 (FRIDAY)

And when they had performed all things according to the law of the Lord, they returned into Galilee, to their own city Nazareth.

—Luke 2:39

For Joseph and Mary, the birth of Jesus was only the beginning. They now faced the monumental task of raising and nurturing the Son of God. Jesus's childhood in Nazareth is a story of hope—hope for a world that will be forever changed by his ministry.

While in Judea, Joseph and Mary diligently observed God's laws and ceremonies. Only then did they journey back to Nazareth. They had remained faithful to the Lord, even far from home, away from their friends, family, and synagogue. They could have lived any way they wanted, but instead, they maintained their genuine faith, respecting and obeying God's teachings for the people of Israel. Their unwavering commitment to God, regardless of location, is an example to all of us.

When Joseph and Mary returned to Nazareth, they faced significant social challenges. In their culture, pregnancy outside of marriage was considered deeply shameful. The townspeople, unaware of the divine nature of Mary's pregnancy, naturally assumed misconduct. This gossip likely persisted for years, potentially affecting the family's standing in the community. Despite Joseph initially planning to divorce Mary quietly (Matthew 1:19), God's intervention led him to stand by her side. The widespread assumption that Joseph was Jesus's father (Luke 3:23) might have mitigated some of the scandals, but whispers likely continued. Through it all, Mary and Joseph's unwavering faith in God's plan shone brightly, setting an example of trust and obedience in the face of societal judgment.

Joseph and Mary made God the center of their home, creating a nurturing environment where Jesus and his siblings flourished in faith. By following God's Law and living right, they built a strong foundation of faith in God for their family.

Teaching Jesus to follow God's Law was very important. Jesus, God in human form, always did what his heavenly Father wanted. As a human child, he had to be trained and taught like other children. When he was old enough to understand and follow the Law, it was apparent to those who knew him that he was the One the prophets had foretold. He lived a perfect life. The Law helped shape Jesus's character as he grew up (Luke 2:52). His obedience to God's Law prepared him for God's plan: to be the sacrifice that would save people.

Jesus grew up and embodied the hope of salvation God had promised through the prophets. Isaiah had foretold, "For unto us a child is born, unto us a son is given and the government shall be upon His shoulder: and His name shall be called Wonderful, Counsellor, The mighty God, The everlasting Father, The Prince of Peace" (Isaiah 9:6). Every day of Jesus's childhood in Nazareth was a step toward fulfilling this prophecy.

As Jesus grew into his preteen years, his life was like other children's in many ways but also very different. He faced all the same sinful temptations as his friends, but Jesus never sinned in his actions, words, or thoughts. Had Jesus never been tempted and learned to resist temptation, he could never say he understood what we go through.

His lessons in dealing with temptation were necessary to become our great High Priest: "For we have not an high priest which cannot be touched with the feeling of our infirmities; but was in all points tempted like as we are, yet without sin" (Hebrews 4:15).

Despite the centuries separating us from ancient Nazareth, modern families can still draw profound wisdom from the timeless principles of Joseph, Mary, and Jesus. The Holy Family's devotion to God illuminates a path for modern households.

Consider the timeless wisdom in Proverbs 22:6: "Train up a child in the way he should go: and when he is old, he will not depart from it." This verse encapsulates the essence of Mary and Joseph's approach to parenting Jesus. They didn't just follow God's rules; they embodied them, creating a living example for their extraordinary child.

Parents can embrace this same calling. By intentionally aligning our family life with biblical teachings, we create an environment where faith can flourish. This isn't about *perfection* but *persistent dedication* to God's ways and modeling a godly life for our children. Just as Jesus matured in wisdom and stature in the humble home of Nazareth, our children, too, can develop spiritually solid roots in homes where God's presence is honored daily.

We can learn to obey God and do what pleases him. Families that pray together, read the Bible, and share the same beliefs help each other get along and grow in grace, making a family stable and content. Despite the world's harshness, families rooted in the faith can thrive.

Families should attend church[53] where the Bible is taught and preached clearly—in a church that stands on Bible principles and will not change or water down God's message. It is encouraging for parents and children to join a fellowship where the members strive to honor Jesus Christ and to live consistent, godly lives.

---

53 "Not forsaking the assembling of ourselves together, as the manner of some is; but exhorting one another: and so much the more, as ye see the day approaching" (Hebrews 10:25).

Joseph and Mary's faithful parenting laid the foundation for Jesus's earthly ministry. Our families currently have a similar, sacred task. We're not just raising children; we're nurturing future disciples.[54] As we strive to follow the example of Jesus's family, we can take comfort in God's promises. Just as he had a plan for Jesus, he also has one for our families. As the prophet Jeremiah reminds us, "For I know the thoughts that I think toward you, saith the Lord, thoughts of peace, and not of evil, to give you an expected end" (Jeremiah 29:11). This verse reassures us that God's plans for his people are ultimately for our good and filled with hope.

After considering the example of Jesus's earthly family and our calling as parents and children, we're reminded that our destination is a heavenly reunion with Jesus Christ. These words, often sung during Christmas, speak to the journey of faith and hope that began in Nazareth and continues in our homes today.

"And our eyes at last shall see Him,
through His own redeeming love;
for that Child so dear and gentle
is our Lord in heav'n above,
and He leads His children on
to the place where He is gone."[55]

---

54 Matthew 28:19a: "Go therefore and make disciples of all nations" (ESV). Parents, should our "disciple-making" not include our own precious children?

55 "Once in Royal David's City," by Cecil Francis Alexander (1848), the third verse. Public domain.

CHAPTER 18

THE CHILD—LUKE 2:40 (SATURDAY)

We can read about Jesus's early years in the Bible, in the book of Luke:

"And the child grew, and waxed strong in spirit, filled with wisdom: and the grace of God was upon Him" (Luke 2:40).

This tells us that Jesus grew up like other children. As he aged, he got bigger and stronger. As Jesus grew, he became a living symbol of hope for all who knew him, foreshadowing the profound impact he would have on humanity.

Yes, Jesus's physical development was much like ours. He had to learn how to walk, first scooting, then crawling and pulling up on things in the house, then finally being brave and letting go of the table and taking those halting steps to Mary. And what do you think Jesus did when he first discovered his shadow? As he grew, he would have had the same teething pains as all babies. Sometime in those first six years, he lost that first baby tooth so his adult teeth could come in.

Jesus probably played familiar children's games of the time. He might have enjoyed knucklebones (like jacks) or hoop rolling with his friends in Nazareth's dusty streets. Jesus's body grew stronger as he made friends with the neighborhood children, played their games, and hiked around the area with the other boys in town. How many times did Jesus stub his toe or skin his knees? Like all children, Jesus may have faced difficult situations. Perhaps he once comforted a friend who had lost a pet or stood up for someone being bullied. One thing is sure: His response to the bully or the pain of childhood boo-boos was never sinful.

When the Bible says Jesus "waxed strong in spirit," it's talking about his heart and mind getting stronger. Just as exercise strengthens our muscles, prayer and learning God's Word strengthened Jesus's spirit. As Jesus grew up, he showed more and more of his perfect kindness, bravery, and faithfulness. He came to understand these qualities more deeply and expressed them in new ways as he matured.

Jesus also grew "in wisdom." The verse says, "And the child grew, and waxed strong in spirit, filled with wisdom . . . " This means that as Jesus got older, his heart and mind became stronger. This experience prepared Jesus to identify with sinners (you and me) in God's plan for humanity's redemption.

Those early walks in the hills with Joseph were tremendous learning opportunities for him. Jesus likely explored the slopes around Nazareth, observing flowers, insects, and birds. Perhaps he marveled at how a tiny seed could grow into a mighty tree, foreshadowing his future teachings about faith. The Creator, as a child, had to learn about his creation. What delight Joseph must have had as he taught Jesus about nature around them.

As the years passed, imagine all the questions about carpentering Jesus had for Joseph as he learned how to drive a nail, bore a hole, and cut a board. Picture Jesus in Joseph's workshop, learning to sand rough wood smooth. He might have made a simple toy or tool under Joseph's watchful eye. Did Joseph show him how to measure twice and cut once? He must have been observant of how his dad gathered the suitable lumber, prepared the wood, shaped the wood, and took special care in smoothing the wooden tools he crafted.

Jesus also learned more about who he was and why he was on earth. He gained this wisdom through:

- His unique relationship with God, his Father in heaven
- Watching and understanding the people around him
- Going through ordinary growing-up experiences

- Studying essential things, especially God's Word, the Torah[56]

Imagine young Jesus sitting cross-legged in the local synagogue, eagerly listening to the rabbi read from the Torah scrolls, his young mind absorbing every word.

As Jesus grew, he understood more about the world and people, helping him prepare for God's plan for his life. Even though Jesus was unique, he still had to learn and grow as we do—he did it without ever doing anything wrong! Amazing!

Jesus, with his family, would have participated in the Jewish festivals. Picture him at the Passover seder, perhaps asking the Four Questions[57]

---

56 The Torah refers to the first five books of the Hebrew Bible, also known as the Pentateuch or the Five Books of Moses. These books are Genesis (Bereshit in Hebrew), Exodus (Shemot), Leviticus (Vayikra), Numbers (Bamidbar), and Deuteronomy (Devarim). The Torah is considered the most sacred text in Judaism and contains the Jewish faith's foundational narratives, laws, and teachings. It covers the creation of the world, the early history of the Jewish people, their exodus from Egypt, and the giving of the law at Mount Sinai.

57 The custom of a child asking questions at the Passover seder was established by the Mishnaic Period (1st-2nd centuries CE), though the form of the questions probably differed from today's. The Four Questions help explain why Passover night is special:

a. "Why unleavened bread?"
   - Reminds of the hasty departure from Egypt
   - "And they baked unleavened cakes of the dough which they brought forth out of Egypt, for it was not leavened; because they were thrust out of Egypt, and could not tarry..." (Exodus 12:39)

b. "Why bitter herbs?"
   - Symbolizes the bitterness of slavery
   - "And they shall eat the flesh in that night, roast with fire, and unleavened bread; and with bitter herbs they shall eat it." (Exodus 12:8, KJV)

c. "Why dip twice?"
   - Represents tears of slavery and sweetness of freedom
   - Custom evolved from: "And ye shall take a bunch of hyssop, and dip it in the blood that is in the bason..." (Exodus 12:22, KJV)

d. "Why recline?"
   - Shows freedom to relax, unlike slaves
   - Reflects God's promise: "I am the Lord, and I will bring you out from under the burdens of the Egyptians..." (Exodus 6:6, KJV)

These questions, typically asked by the youngest person present, help retell the Exodus story and its significance.

as the youngest male. His young voice filled with curiosity about the significance of this sacred meal.

The Bible also says, "The grace of God was upon Him." This means God's love and kindness were with Jesus from the start. God's grace was a gentle cover, wrapping the child in warmth and favor. This love from God helped his Son Jesus grow up well. This divine grace was not just for Jesus but a promise of hope for all humanity—a glimpse of coming salvation.

Another part of the Bible talks about this too. It says, "And the Word [*Jesus*] was made flesh [*the Incarnation*] and dwelt among us, (and we beheld his glory, the glory as of the only begotten of the Father,) full of grace and truth" (John 1:14). This shows how much God loved Jesus and how Jesus came to earth and shared that love with others.

Jesus's childhood is a blueprint for our own lives today. Jesus showed us that growing up is about more than just our bodies changing. It's about developing our minds, hearts, and relationship with God. Jesus's growth gives us hope that we, too, can develop in wisdom and favor with God. As we've seen how Jesus grew, we might wonder, "What does this mean for me?" Jesus didn't just grow up to be an example—he grew up to be our Savior. And because of that, we have a choice to make. We can follow Jesus and grow like he did or go our own way and face disastrous consequences. Let's think very carefully about what choice we want to make.

God wants to give us his grace too! Grace means getting something good that we didn't earn. That's what salvation is: *a gift of grace*. The Bible says, "For by grace are ye saved through faith; and that not of yourselves: it is the gift of God: Not of works, lest any man should boast" (Ephesians 2:8–9). This means we cannot do anything to earn God's love or salvation. Grace is undeserved. We can have this *free gift*, as God enables us to understand what Jesus did for us. Then, by faith, we can place our trust in Jesus's work alone to save us.

As children of God, this grace helps us grow and become more like him. It's impressive that God has the same kind of love for us that he has for his Son!

Jesus's childhood wasn't just about his personal growth—it was the beginning of hope for all of us. His development prepared him for his ultimate role as our Savior, the source of eternal life.

Now here's something important to think about:

If you haven't yet, you can ask Jesus to be your Savior. He grew up to save us from our sins and give us a new life with God. If you already know Jesus, keep growing as he did! Strengthen your faith by reading his Word daily. Continue to grow in your relationship with God, and let his Word, the Bible, guide you.

Remember, Jesus, the God-man, came to earth as a baby in Bethlehem and grew up to be our Savior. His story can change our lives today. As we reflect on Jesus's childhood, remember that his growth was the *Dawning of Hope* for the world. Each step he took, each lesson he learned, brought us closer to the hope of salvation.

We've seen how Jesus grew in body, mind, and spirit. But what about us? How can we grow to be more like Jesus? Let's close our chapter with a short poem. It's from a song, a prayer to Jesus, asking for help to grow righteously. As you read it, think about making these words your prayer:

"Teach me how to grow in goodness,
daily as I grow;
Thou hast been a child, and surely
thou dost know."[58]

This simple prayer reminds us that Jesus understands what it is like to be a child. He knows how to help us grow in goodness, just as he did. Let's carry these words in our hearts as we try to grow more like Jesus daily.

---

58 "Jesus, Friend of All the Children," by Walter John Mathams, the second verse. Public domain.

FOURTH WEEK SCRIPTURE READING (SUNDAY)

Now his parents went to Jerusalem every year at the feast of the Passover. And when he was twelve years old, they went up to Jerusalem after the custom of the feast. And when they had fulfilled the days, as they returned, the child Jesus tarried behind in Jerusalem; and Joseph and his mother knew not of it. But they, supposing him to have been in the company, went a day's journey; and they sought him among their kinsfolk and acquaintance. And when they found him not, they turned back again to Jerusalem, seeking him. And it came to pass, that after three days they found him in the temple, sitting in the midst of the doctors, both hearing them, and asking them questions. And all that heard him were astonished at his understanding and answers. And when they saw him, they were amazed: and his mother said unto him, "Son, why hast thou thus dealt with us? behold, thy father and I have sought thee sorrowing." And he said unto them, "How is it that ye sought me? wist ye not that I must be about my Father's business?" And they understood not the saying which he spake unto them.

And he went down with them, and came to Nazareth, and was subject unto them: but his mother kept all these sayings in her heart. And Jesus increased in wisdom and stature, and in favor with God and man.

—Luke 2:41–52

CHAPTER 19

THE PANIC—LUKE 2:41–45 (MONDAY)

Now his parents went to Jerusalem every year at the feast of the Passover. And when he was twelve years old, they went up to Jerusalem after the custom of the feast. And when they had fulfilled the days, as they returned, the child Jesus tarried behind in Jerusalem, and Joseph and his mother knew not of it. But they, supposing him to have been in the company, went a day's journey, and they sought him among their kinsfolk and acquaintance. And when they found him not, they turned back again to Jerusalem, seeking him.

—Luke 2:41–45

As Joseph, Mary, and Jesus journeyed to Jerusalem, an air of eager anticipation surrounded them. The Passover feast wasn't just a celebration of the past but also a monument to enduring hope. It reminded the people of God's faithfulness and promises yet to be fulfilled.

For Mary and Joseph, this hope took on a special significance. Jesus embodied the joining of heavenly promises and earthly hope—a child with a divine calling. As they watched him grow, their hearts swelled with wonder and hope, sensing that his life would fulfill the ancient prophecies whispered through generations. Little did they know that this Passover journey would test their faith and deepen their understanding of the hope they carried.

The Passover celebration had been especially meaningful this year. As Jesus participated fully for the first time as a young man of twelve, Joseph and Mary watched with thankfulness and awe, their hope in his purpose renewed. As they began their journey home, their hearts were full of the feast's significance and the joy of shared worship.

The sun dipped low on the horizon as Mary, Joseph, and their friends from Nazareth were ending their first day of travel, heading back home from the annual Feast of Passover in Jerusalem. The bustling crowd was alive with joy, and the celebration echoed through the air.

So many memories must have been stirred in Joseph and Mary as they recalled walking home on this road for the first time together with baby Jesus. It was a dozen or so years earlier, but it seemed like yesterday. Yet amid the laughter and chatter of the travelers, a silent storm began brewing within Mary's heart. Their joy was about to be eclipsed by a shadow that Mary and Joseph had never anticipated.

As the group walked on, recounting the moments of the feast, Mary noticed an unsettling absence in their company. Jesus, their twelve-year-old son, was not among them. The knot tightened in her stomach. The looks of concern that were exchanged between Mary and Joseph spoke volumes. Panic seized their hearts as they realized their precious child was not in the familiar circle of travelers.

They desperately questioned family and friends who had journeyed with them. "Have you seen Jesus?" But the answers were always the same: no sign of him anywhere. No one had seen him since they left the city early that morning!

As worry tightened its grip, Mary and Joseph clung desperately to God's promises about Jesus. Their fear of losing him battled with their hope in his divine purpose. "Surely," Mary thought, "the child of prophecy couldn't simply vanish." Their anxious search was punctuated by moments of reassurance as they recalled the angel's words and the miracles surrounding Jesus's birth.

"Where could he be?" Joseph wondered, his heart racing. Then, a quiet voice of hope whispered, "Remember what God said about him." Fear and faith wrestled within as they retraced their steps.

Anxiety clung to them like a heavy cloak as they realized the seriousness of the situation. "Our Jesus is missing and alone in the city!" The thought drove them on to Jerusalem quicker than they had ever traveled this road before. When they finally arrived, the city was quiet. Those streets, recently filled with celebration, now only echoed with their frantic calls for their missing son.

Their search felt like navigating a stormy sea. Waves of fear threatened to overwhelm them, but the lighthouse of God's promises kept piercing through the darkness, guiding them on.

They may have wondered, "How could we lose our precious boy?" or "Why didn't we do more to protect him?" In Joseph and Mary's frantic searching, they may have remembered David's cry in Psalms when he was in trouble: "Thy face, Lord, will I seek" (Psalm 27:8). Have you noticed how often the Lord reminds us of statements in his Word that calm our souls during a crisis? Hopefully, like Joseph and Mary, we will quickly turn to the Lord.

Prayer marked their search. Whispered through trembling lips, they beseeched God for the safety of their beloved child. The narrow streets seemed longer, the shadows darker, as they retraced the path they had just walked. Despite their growing dread, Joseph and Mary's search remained methodical. Their trust in God's promises gave them clarity amid the chaos, helping them think of places where Jesus might be found.

As night fell, Mary recalled her fear of fleeing to Egypt and how God had protected them then. This memory rekindled her hope, tempering her fear with trust in divine protection.

This story from Jesus's childhood has sage implications for God's children today. In our modern world, losing sight of Jesus can be as simple as getting caught up in the noise of social media, the demands of work, or the distractions of entertainment. This incident reminds us that we can carelessly forget the very One we say we "worship." This often happens in all the hurry and activity of the Christmas season. We may need to reexamine our priorities, such as Mary and Joseph retracing their steps.

With all our Christmas celebrations and routines, may we always keep our eyes on Jesus in the hectic rush of life. Let our hearts echo the psalmist's words: "As the [deer] panteth after the water brooks, So panteth my soul after thee, O God" (Psalm 42:1). May our pursuit of God remain fervent and unwavering, even during business, panic, and uncertainty.

As we journey through this season, may we, like Mary and Joseph, move from panic to peace, from searching to finding, always holding onto the hope that defines our faith. The Christ child they sought in Jerusalem is the same Christ who seeks us, inviting us daily into a deeper relationship with him.

"Prone to wander, Lord, I feel it,
Prone to leave the God I love.
Here's my heart, O take and seal it,
Seal it for Thy courts above."[59]

---

59 "Come, Thou Fount of Every Blessing," by Robert Robinson (1758), the last lines of the third verse. Public domain.

CHAPTER 20

THE AMAZEMENT—LUKE 2:46–51 (TUESDAY)

Joseph and Mary, Jesus's earthly parents, had made an unsettling discovery! Jesus was not in the company of friends and relatives traveling home from the Feast of the Passover in Jerusalem. No one had seen him, and his parents panicked as they looked everywhere in the city for him. While initially causing distress, this event would ultimately bring them hope and a deeper understanding of Jesus's divine nature:

And it came to pass that after three days, they found him in the temple, sitting in the midst of the doctors, both hearing them and asking them questions. And all that heard him were astonished at his understanding and answers. And when they saw him, they were amazed: and his mother said unto him, "Son, why hast thou thus dealt with us? Behold, thy father and I have sought thee sorrowing." And he said unto them, "How is it that ye sought me? Wist ye not that I must be about my Father's business?" And they understood not the saying which he spake unto them. And he went down with them, and came to Nazareth, and was subject unto them: but his mother kept all these sayings in her heart. (Luke 2:46–51)

The Scriptures recount this event, revealing that after three days of worried searching, his parents finally found Jesus in the Temple, sitting among the learned teachers, listening to them, and asking questions. They knew their twelve-year-old better than anyone, yet they were surprised to see and listen to him here.

We might wonder why Joseph and Mary didn't look in the Temple first. Perhaps they, like many of us, didn't immediately consider that Jesus would be engaged in spiritual matters. This reminds us how easy it is to overlook the obvious in our lives. How often do we search for answers, for purpose, for God himself, in all the wrong places before turning to his Word and prayer?

Their three-day search parallels our own journeys. We sometimes spend days, months, or even years looking for meaning and direction in our lives, forgetting to seek God first. Jesus later taught, "Seek ye first the kingdom of God" (Matthew 6:33), a lesson his parents learned firsthand in this experience.

Yet this story also offers hope. When Joseph and Mary finally sought Jesus in the right place, they found him. This echoes the promise Jesus would later make: "*Ask, and it shall be given you; seek, and ye shall find; knock, and it shall be opened unto you: For every one that asketh receiveth; and he that seeketh findeth; and to him that knocketh it shall be opened*" (Matthew 7:7–8). No matter how long or where we've searched, when we turn to God, he is there, ready to welcome us into a deeper understanding of his purpose for our lives.

Luke's words unfold with Mary expressing her concern to Jesus, "*Son, why have you treated us so? Behold, your father and I have been searching for you in great anguish.*" Jesus responded with a question that reveals his divine awareness: "*Why were you looking for me? Didn't you know I must be doing my Father's Business?*" This statement highlights Jesus's early understanding of his unique relationship with God.

This exchange clues us to essential truths about Jesus and offers timeless lessons for parents and growing believers today. The episode reveals Jesus's early awareness of his divine identity and mission. Even at the tender age of twelve, he understood the priority of being in communion with his heavenly Father. Jesus's early awareness of his divine mission brings hope to believers, demonstrating that God's plan of salvation was unfolding, even in Christ's youth. This shows how important it is for believers to build a close relationship with God from a young age.

Today, teaching our children the claims of Christ from the Scriptures should begin early in their lives. Jesus's example gives us hope that we, also, will be able to grow in wisdom and favor with God, regardless of our age or background.

Additionally, Jesus showed humility by listening and asking questions, showing his desire to learn. This challenges us to approach our spiritual journey with a similar attitude of seeking and learning. In Proverbs, we are encouraged to incline our hearts to wisdom and apply our hearts to understanding (Proverbs 2:1–5; see verse 2), reinforcing the value of a humble and teachable spirit.

This experience helped Joseph and Mary better understand God's plan for Jesus. Parents can find hope in this story, knowing that God has a unique purpose for each child, just as he did for Jesus. The narrative calls on parents today to recognize and nurture unique qualities and godly purposes as they are observed in their children.

For growing believers, Jesus's example urges us to prioritize our relationship with God. We must recognize the importance of daily hearing him speak to us through his Word, communing with him in prayer, and maintaining an attitude of humility throughout our spiritual journey. As we go through good and bad times in life, we are reminded to seek wisdom and understanding from the Word of God, following the example set by Jesus in his formative years.

This event—Jesus in the Temple—shows us many things. It reveals God's plan. It shows how amazed his parents were. It also teaches us how to follow Jesus's example with our faith. It shows parents that each child has a particular purpose. It encourages believers to be humble in their faith, consistently seeking wisdom in the presence of our heavenly Father.

The hymn "Trust and Obey" captures the spirit of Jesus's example. It reminds us that following God's way, like Jesus did, brings joy and blessing to our lives.

"Not a burden we bear,
not a sorrow we share,
but our toil He doth richly repay;
not a grief or a loss,
not a frown or a cross,
but is blest if we trust and obey.

"Trust and obey, for there's no other way
to be happy in Jesus, but to trust and obey."[60]

As we reflect on young Jesus in the Temple, let these words inspire us to trust God's plan and obey his guidance.

---

60 "Trust and Obey," by John H. Sammis (1887), second verse and refrain. Public domain.

CHAPTER 21

THE WISDOM—LUKE 2:52A (WEDNESDAY)

And Jesus increased in wisdom . . .

—Luke 2:52a

As Jesus grew up, Mary often marveled at her extraordinary son. Even when he was young, Jesus showed wisdom far beyond his age. God inspired Luke to share a brief but powerful glimpse into Jesus's childhood. Luke wrote: *"And Jesus increased in wisdom and stature, and in favor with God and man"* (Luke 2:52). This short sentence tells much about Jesus's early years.

The Bible shows us something amazing—Jesus, who is completely God and completely man, the God-man, chose to become a helpless baby. Despite his divine nature, Jesus's decision to grow in wisdom as a human was intentional. He chose to fully identify with our human experience, including the process of learning and maturing. This demonstrates both his humility and his desire to relate to us completely.

Before his Incarnation, Jesus was already God and all-knowing.[61] Even before Creation, we can read of Jesus, "In the beginning was the Word [*Jesus*], and the Word was with God, and the Word was God" (John 1:1).

---

61 How could Jesus, who is all-knowing God, grow in wisdom? The answer lies in the mystery of the Incarnation. While never ceasing to be God, Jesus, taking on human flesh, fully embraced the human experience, including the process of learning and maturing in understanding.

Proverbs 8 hints that he was there when the world was made. In fact, Jesus is our Creator. As it says in Colossians, "For by Him were all things created, that are in heaven, and that are in earth, visible and invisible, whether *they be* thrones, or dominions, or principalities, or powers: all things were created by Him, and for Him" (Colossians 1:16).

Jesus Christ purposefully designed everything in the universe, from the biggest star to the tiniest microbe. With his amazing intelligence, he created everything just by speaking. He even gave Adam, the first man, the ability to think and apply wisdom.

Jesus knows everything! The Bible tells us that "all the treasures of wisdom and knowledge" are found in him (Colossians 2:3). This means that even as a baby in the manger, Jesus wasn't just another child—he was God's wisdom in human form.

Even though Jesus was God, he chose to lay aside some of his divine abilities for a time. This allowed him to experience growth like a human child. As a baby, he made happy noises and cried, seeing the world as any baby would. The One who created wisdom chose to experience growing wise through his development as a human being.

Jesus's growing wisdom teaches us important lessons as parents and believers. We specialize in helping our children grow smarter, stronger in faith, and more emotionally mature. Mary was amazed as she watched Jesus grow and learn. We, too, should see how special each child is and help them grow into unique adults.

The Bible talks about two different kinds of wisdom. First, there's "worldly wisdom," which James in the Bible calls "**this** Wisdom" (James 3:15). This kind of "earthly wisdom" is not real—this fake wisdom is selfish and harmful and goes against what God wants. It's what people sometimes call being "streetwise."

Then, James talks about "**the** Wisdom" (James 3:17). This is God's true wisdom, "wisdom from above." It comes from God's Word, the Bible. This type of wisdom is good, peaceful, and kind. It helps us to think right and live right. This is the kind of wisdom Jesus had, and "**the** wisdom" is what we should grow in and teach our children. The godly wisdom Jesus exemplified offers hope in a world filled with confusion and despair.

This Wisdom	*The* Wisdom
Selfish	Selfless
Shortsighted	Eternal perspective
Leads to conflict	Promotes peace
Earthly focused	Heavenly focused
Fake!	*Real!*

As we live our lives and wait for Jesus to come back, let's keep learning from his endless wisdom. Jesus, whom the Bible calls "the Word made flesh," grew in wisdom. If we follow him, he'll teach us what's true—the truth that lasts forever.

As we grow in wisdom like Jesus did, we gain hope for the future. Understanding God's ways gives us confidence in his plans and promises. The wisdom Jesus embodied and grew in is the same wisdom that gives us hope as we await his Second Coming. It helps us understand God's plan and trust in his wise timing.

"My wisdom and my guide,
My Counsellor thou art;
O never let me leave thy side,
Or from thy paths depart!"[62]

---

62 Wesley, Charles, "Jesus, My Truth, My Way," the second stanza. Public domain.

CHAPTER 22

THE STATURE—LUKE 2:52B (THURSDAY)

And Jesus increased in . . . stature . . .

—Luke 2:52b

Luke describes Jesus's growth:

"*And Jesus increased in wisdom and stature, and in favor with God and man*" (Luke 2:52).

This helps us understand how Jesus grew from a baby born in a stable to an adult. It shows us that Jesus grew up just like us, even though he was God's Son. His physical growth gives us hope, showing that God understands our journey from childhood to adulthood.

Jesus had two natures—he was entirely God and fully human. As God, he had all of God's attributes (divine abilities). But as a human, he was limited to a body and mind that grew and learned like ours. These two natures were joined together in one person: Jesus. This means that Jesus could do things only God can do, but he also felt hunger, pain, and emotions like we do.

He had a natural human body with all its limits but without sin. The "hands" of the Creator who made the stars and planets had to learn how to grasp things. The "eyes" that saw the world being made had to get used to the bright sunlight in Bethlehem. The all-knowing mind of God experienced human learning and development.

Jesus experienced the physical changes and challenges we all face as we develop from infancy to adulthood. He went through all the growing-up stages: infant, child, teenager, and adult. The Bible tells us that Jesus "was in all points tempted like as we are, yet without sin" (Hebrews 4:15). This means Jesus truly understands what growing up is like.

Jesus's willingness to grow up as a human being shows his humility and gives us hope. His life shows us how to live and reminds us that we can grow and improve at every stage.

Jesus's journey from baby to adult fills us with hopefulness. As we think about Jesus growing up, we can have hope for our growth. Just as he increased in stature, with his help, we, too, can grow stronger in body and spirit.

Because physical growth is essential, we should remember to care for our bodies. While the Bible emphasizes that spiritual growth is most important, it also recognizes the value of physical health (1 Timothy 4:8; Hebrews 4:15; 3 John 1:2).

Let's let these wise words from the Bible encourage wise use of our bodies.

The Apostle Paul tells us, "What? know ye not that your body is the temple of the Holy Ghost which is in you, which ye have of God, and ye are not your own? For ye are bought with a price: therefore glorify God in your body, and in your spirit, which are God's" (1 Corinthians 6:19–20).

Solomon, the wise king, said, "Be not wise in thine own eyes: Fear the Lord and depart from evil. It shall be health to thy navel And marrow to thy bones" (Proverbs 3:7–8).

And Paul, once again, shows how keeping the body in control keeps a believer fit for service: "But I keep under my body and bring it into subjection: lest that by any means, when I have preached to others, I myself should be a castaway" (1 Corinthians 9:27).

The all-powerful God willingly became a growing child to thoroughly experience what we do. Imagine the Creator of all things experiencing the awkwardness of puberty, the excitement of mastering new skills, and the challenges of maturing. Why? So that He could connect with us completely at every age and stage of life.

"He came down to earth from heaven
who is God and Lord of all,
and His shelter was a stable,
and His cradle was a stall:
with the poor, and meek, and lowly,
lived on earth our Savior holy."[63]

---

63 "Once in Royal David's City," by Cecil Francis Alexander (1848), the second verse. Public domain.

CHAPTER 23

THE SPIRIT—LUKE 2:52C (FRIDAY)

And Jesus increased . . . in favor with God.

—Luke 2:52c

During Advent, we learn something amazing and hopeful: Jesus grew spiritually! This idea might surprise us, but it's essential to Christ's growth. It shows us the maturing of his human side, giving us a notable example of how to grow spiritually.

Luke relates: "*And Jesus increased in wisdom and stature, and in favor with God and man*" (Luke 2:52). This short sentence shows us that Jesus grew in many ways—physically, mentally, spiritually, and socially. Every part of His growth had a purpose: to prepare him for his important work in the world.

But why did Jesus, the God-man, need to grow spiritually? The answer to this question helps us understand the mystery of Jesus becoming human. Even though Jesus was always God, he chose to fully experience life as a human, including growing and learning. He didn't do this because he lacked anything as God, but he wanted to identify with us in every way as a man.

Before God made the world, Jesus already existed. He was always with God the Father and the Holy Spirit—they are the three persons of One God.[64] When Jesus came to earth as a baby, he became fully human while still being fully God. This is hard for us to understand completely, but it's important.

---

64 God as the "three in One" is known as *the Trinity*. We could say he is a *tri-unity*.

Jesus didn't just appear human or pretend to be human. He was truly and fully human, experiencing everything we do—growing, learning, feeling hungry and tired. At the same time, he never stopped being fully God. He was both at once—fully God and fully human.

Jesus completely took on human nature while retaining his divine nature. This is a profound mystery that goes beyond simple comparisons.

This amazing truth shows how much God loves us—he became one of us to save us while still being God. It helps us understand how Jesus could be both God and a human who grew and learned, experiencing life just as we do.

Jesus's growth gives us hope in several ways. First, it shows us that he understands what being human is like. Because Jesus grew up just like we do, he knows the challenges we face at every age.

Second, Jesus's growth shows us how we can grow spiritually. Just as he grew in wisdom and favor with God, we can also grow in our understanding and relationship with God. This growth isn't about earning God's love—we already have that in Jesus—but about getting to know God better.

The Bible gives us glimpses of how Jesus grew spiritually. In the Gospels, we see him spending time alone with God, worshiping regularly, and learning the Scriptures well. We can follow his example in these things.

Jesus's baptism was an important moment in his spiritual journey. When he came out of the water, God's voice said, "This is my beloved Son, in whom I am well pleased" (Matthew 3:17). This showed that God approved of his Son Jesus and how he had grown before starting his public ministry.

As we think about Jesus's growth, we're reminded to grow spiritually too. The Apostle Paul describes this: "I am crucified with Christ: nevertheless I live; yet not I, but Christ liveth in me: and the life which I now live in the flesh I live by the faith of the Son of God, who loved me and gave himself for me" (Galatians 2:20). Our spiritual growth happens as we "grow in grace, and in the knowledge of our Lord and Savior Jesus Christ" (2 Peter 3:18).

We can grow spiritually also because God gives us the power to do so. When we turn away from our sins and put our trust in Jesus, we're forgiven and become part of God's family. From then on, we start a lifelong journey of becoming more like Jesus. This involves choosing God's way instead of our own, learning from the Bible, and getting closer to God.

The goal of our spiritual growth is to hear God say to us what the Master said to the faithful servant in Jesus's parable: "Well done, good and faithful servant . . . enter thou into the joy of thy lord" (Matthew 25:23). We don't earn this by being perfect but by faithfully growing and serving God.

In this season of waiting and preparing, let Jesus's growth inspire us to grow spiritually. Let's do the things that help our faith grow, like reading the Bible, praying, listening to godly preaching, and helping others. We can trust that God will help us in this growth. As the Bible says, "Being confident of this very thing, that he which hath begun a good work in you will perform it until the day of Jesus Christ" (Philippians 1:6). God, who started helping us grow, will keep helping us until the end.

As we grow more like Jesus, people around us can see the notable changes that happen when someone follows Christ. This brings hope to a world that desperately needs it.

> "O come, O Wisdom from on high,
> who ordered all things mightily;
> to us, the path of knowledge show
> and teach us in its ways to go.
> Rejoice! Rejoice! Immanuel
> shall come to you, O Israel."[65]

---

65 "O Come, O Come, Emmanuel," Latin from the 12th century. Translator: J. M. Neale (1851). The second verse. Public domain.

CHAPTER 24

THE COMMUNITY—LUKE 2:52D (SATURDAY)

And Jesus increased . . . in favor with . . . man.

—Luke 2:52d

As Jesus's life on earth unfolds, each of the Gospels shows us something about him. This final chapter examines Luke's last important truth about Jesus's First Coming, showing how Jesus grew in his relationships with people.

Luke tells us how Jesus grew: "*And Jesus increased in wisdom and stature, and in favor with God and man*" (Luke 2:52). This shows that Jesus grew in body, wisdom, and relationships with God and people.

Jesus had to learn how to communicate with people to teach and help them. Even though Jesus was God's Son, the Creator, as a human being, he still had to learn how to live with people on earth. Jesus felt our limitations, including how hard it can be to get along with others.

Jesus observed and learned from his interactions with people throughout his earthly life. When he was in Jerusalem for Passover and did miracles, "many believed" in him. But Jesus was careful with these phony "believers" because he knew how quickly people can change their minds. John says that Jesus didn't trust himself to them because he knew what was in each person (John 2:23–25).

People liked Jesus's miracles, but some turned away when he started teaching (John 6). He knew what was in their hearts, which helped him care for them wisely and recognize what they needed.

As we wait for Jesus to come again, we should think about what his growth in relationships means for us. The Bible shows us that Jesus was kind, even to those rejected by society, like tax collectors and sinners. He cared for people who were suffering and left out (Matthew 9:36; Mark 1:40–41).

The Gospels give us many examples of how Jesus treated others. He was very patient with his disciples, even when they doubted or made mistakes. He kept teaching them, even when they didn't understand, showing how committed he was to helping them grow (Mark 8:17–21; Luke 24:25–27).

Jesus tells us to love people the same way he loves us (John 13:34). His love for people was evident when he healed sick people, forgave sins (Luke 23:34; Matthew 18:21–22), or spent time with outcasts (John 13:34). The Bible shows us Jesus's kindness to others (John 11:35; Luke 10:21), his serving (Matthew 20:28), his friendship (John 15:15; Luke 24:14–23), his bravery (Matthew 23:13–36; Mark 2:1–12), his wisdom (Matthew 22:15–22; John 4:7–26), and most of all, his humility (Philippians 2:5–8).

Jesus even showed us what righteous anger looks like. He wasn't angry when people were mean to him, but he was angry when people were mean to others or when they disrespected God's house and insulted his Father (Matthew 21:12–13).

Dear child of God, shouldn't we try to treat others as well as Jesus has treated us?

In chapter 2, Luke reveals that Jesus the God-Man learned in isolation and within the fabric of community life. Jesus talked to all kinds of people—his family, neighbors, followers, religious leaders, and outcasts. He welcomed everyone, questioned unfair rules, and was kind to those in need (Matthew 9:36; Mark 1:40–41). Mark echoes this sentiment (Mark

2:17), underscoring Jesus's mission to heal not the healthy but the sick—a poignant reminder of our calling to reach out to the lost and broken.

We should try to emulate Jesus's heart in how we treat others. God wants us to honor him by helping others in need (1 Corinthians 10:3 1–33). Like Jesus, we should be discerning in our relationships and show kindness to everyone. We should welcome different kinds of people, challenge society's rules that contradict God's truth, and be kind to people whom others ignore.

Jesus came to earth, lived without sin, told everyone the Good News, died for our sins, came back to life after three days, went back to his Father, and is preparing a place for us. As we wait for Jesus to return, let's live by his teachings and share his love and hope with others who need it.

"The Savior of all people
has brought His peace to you;
now go and tell the story,
for others need it, too.

"To ev'ry land and nation
ring out the gospel call;
proclaim that Christ is risen
and grants His peace to all.

"I love to tell the story;
'twill be my theme in glory
to tell the old, old story
of Jesus and His love."[66]

---

66 "I Love to Tell the Story," by Kate Hankey (1866); author of the refrain by William G. Fischer (1869), seventh verse and refrain. Public domain.

EPILOGUE

As we close the pages of this book, the echoes of angelic songs still linger in our ears. We can almost feel the rough straw of the manger and smell the earthy scent of the stable where Jesus was born. The story of Christ's birth and early years fills our hearts with wonder and hope.

Thank you, dear reader, for journeying with us through these chapters. We've witnessed the miracle of God becoming flesh, felt Mary and Joseph's love for their special child, and marveled at the faith of humble shepherds and wise men.

Just as the star guided those seekers to Jesus, may this story guide you closer to him. Jesus grew from that helpless baby into the God-man who brought salvation to all peoples. His teachings of love, salvation, forgiveness, and compassion continue to inspire us today.

As you go forward, remember the lessons from Jesus's early life:

- *Be humble*, like the simple stable where he was born.
- *Have faith*, like Mary and Joseph, trusting God's plan.
- *Seek wisdom*, like the wise old Simeon and Anna portrayed.
- *Share the Good News*, like the shepherds spreading joy.

As we conclude this part of Jesus's life story, two profound observations emerge, offering valuable insights into the nature of faith and obedience.

First, we encounter a beautiful trait in Mary, the mother of Jesus. After his birth, amid the angelic display and the shepherds' worship, we read, "But Mary kept all these things, and pondered them in her heart" (Luke 2:19). Years later, following the incident where Joseph and Mary find Jesus in the Temple, we find a similar sentiment: "But his mother kept all these sayings in her heart" (Luke 2:51).

Mary's habit of treasuring these moments is more than mere sentimentality. It offers us hope, reminding us to look for God's handiwork in our daily lives, knowing that he is always at work. In a world that often rushes from one moment to the next, Mary's example encourages us to pause, reflect, and recognize the divine fingerprints on the pages of our lives.

Then, we turn our attention to our genuinely exceptional Lord Jesus. After his time in his "Father's house," he humbly returns to Nazareth with his earthly parents. The Scripture succinctly describes the next eighteen years of Jesus's life until he was thirty: "And he went down with them, and came to Nazareth, and was subject unto them" (Luke 2:51).

Pause for a moment and consider the magnitude of this statement. The King of kings, the Lord of all creation, submits himself to imperfect human adults for eighteen more years! This profound act of humility exemplifies Christ's character and provides believers with a powerful model of obedience.

Dear child of God, note that Jesus did this without any gripe or complaint! We will always do well in our Christian lives when we follow Jesus's example closely. His willingness to submit to earthly authorities gives us hope that we, too, can find purpose and divine approval in our everyday obedience.

Jesus's time in the Temple teaches us important lessons. We see his wisdom, focus on God's work, and obedience to his earthly parents. Like Mary, we can treasure these truths in our hearts. Just as Jesus was about his Father's business, we, too, can be busy doing God's will for our lives. And like Jesus's return to Nazareth, we can humbly obey those in authority over us.

I'd like to offer a challenge for the upcoming year:

My memory is not that good. How about yours? Because of this, journaling is an excellent habit to develop. Recording what God does for us and what he teaches us from his Word provides a resource that will help us remember his gracious work in our lives. Just as Mary kept and pondered these things in her heart, we, too, can create a tangible record of God's faithfulness, wisdom, and love in our journey.

We align ourselves with Christ's example by treasuring our moments, focusing on God's will, and cultivating humble obedience. May we, like Jesus, grow in wisdom and stature and favor with God and man.

Let's strive to become more like Jesus every day. His story doesn't end here—it's just the beginning! In the next book of our "Hope" series, Lord willing, we'll explore Jesus's incredible life, his powerful ministry, and the greatest miracle of all—his death and resurrection. *The Dawn of Hope* we've seen here will grow into a brilliant light for all the world. Until then, may the peace and love of Christ fill your heart, not just at Christmas but all year through.

Grace to you,

Joe Henson

I have a free gift for you: a downloadable Bible Study Journal. Use it to study the Bible for the 24 days of Advent leading up to Christmas.

Go to the website below to pick up your free gift.

[Sign up with this URL – https://projecthope. hensonpublishing.com]

ACKNOWLEDGMENTS

I thank my God upon every remembrance of you.

—Philippians 1:3

As I reflect on the journey that led to the creation of *The Dawn of Hope*, the words of the Apostle Paul in Philippians 1:3 resonate deeply with me. His expression of gratitude is a sentiment I share, as I am deeply thankful to the many individuals who have been instrumental in bringing this work to fruition. Their support and influence have been invaluable, and I am forever grateful for their contributions. Their efforts have not only made this book a reality but have also enriched the lives of its readers, making a significant impact on those who seek hope and inspiration.

First and foremost, I must express my deepest gratitude to my beloved wife, Garthea. For over four decades, you have been the quiet voice urging me to put pen to paper, believing in my ability to share our story long before I did. Your patient encouragement finally blossomed into action, and this book is as much a product of your perseverance as it is of my writing. You have been my unwavering support, sounding board, and anchor throughout this journey. Your belief in me and this project has been a constant source of inspiration, pushing me forward when doubts crept in. More than just a supportive presence, you have given me insightful editorial suggestions that have shaped and refined these pages in countless ways. Garthea, your fingerprints are on every word, every idea, and every emotion captured in this book. This work is a testament to our partnership, and I am deeply grateful for your love, patience, and wisdom, which have made *The Dawn of Hope* a reality. Without you, this book would not be what it is today.

I owe a debt of gratitude to my father, Dr. Joe Henson, who wore many hats in my life—father, mentor, and teacher. As my philosophy of science professor at Bob Jones University in 1976, you issued a challenge that has echoed through the decades: for young preachers in the making to become writers, "defending the faith." Daddy, your words planted a seed that has taken nearly half a century to fully germinate. I've never forgotten that challenge, and I wonder if you ever imagined that I would one day pick up the gauntlet you threw down. This book is a testament to the enduring power of your influence and the weight your words carried. Your mentorship has not only shaped my writing but has also guided my life's journey. Thank you for believing in the potential of your students and your son to make a difference through the written word.

I am also grateful to my son Joseph, a pastor-teacher-writer whose own journey has been a source of inspiration and challenge for me. Joseph, watching you work tirelessly at your craft over the years has helped to motivate me to put my ideas into writing. Your dedication to the written word, evident in your many sacred songs, devotional blogs, and pulpit ministry, is a testament to your deep love for the Lord. The beauty and depth of your writing spring from your consistent study of God's Word, enriching both your writing and preaching. You are, in every sense, a genuine wordsmith.

Alongside Joseph, I must also acknowledge his sweet wife, Kristi. Your talents as a writer and counselor complement Joseph's gifts beautifully, creating a formidable team in both ministry and life. Thank you, Joseph and Kristi, for setting such an example and challenging me through your faithfulness to share our faith through this book. Keep on writing, Bubba!

I am grateful to Carly Catt and her exceptional editing team. Your patient guidance and expertise were invaluable as I navigated the challenging waters of converting my ideas into coherent prose. As this is my first attempt at writing for a broader audience, your gentle critiques and insightful suggestions improved the manuscript and helped me grow as a writer. Carly, your ability to see the potential in my raw thoughts and your commitment to helping me refine them into their best possible form has been nothing short of transformative. I sincerely appreciate you and your team for your dedication, keen eyes, and unwavering support throughout this journey.

I am deeply indebted to two individuals who played crucial roles as beta readers: my pastor, Brandon Joyner, and my daughter-in-law Becky Henson. Your contributions to this work have been invaluable and deeply personal.

Pastor Brandon, your kind and positive words have been a blessing. Your encouragement to boldly share our story while remaining grounded in faith has been a source of inspiration.

Becky, your keen editorial eye has been priceless in my writing. As a family member and a skilled reader, you brought a unique perspective that helped bridge the gap between personal experience and universal truth. Your suggestions have polished this narrative, making it more accessible and impactful for readers, and the occasional cinnamon rolls were greatly appreciated!

To both of you, I extend my heartfelt gratitude. Your insightful feedback, unwavering support, and many words of encouragement have left an indelible mark on this book. You've helped shape the words and the heart of *The Dawn of Hope*. This book is richer and more meaningful because of your contributions, and I am thankful for your investment in this project.

Thanks to Karen Piña, my book publishing coach, whose expertise and guidance were instrumental in bringing this book to life. Karen, your insight into self-publishing and your unwavering support throughout this process has been invaluable. You took me under your wing and patiently guided me through each step of this journey, turning what could have been an overwhelming process into an exciting adventure.

I also want to express my heartfelt gratitude to Kurt Bubna and the entire team at Selfpublishing.com. Your professionalism, expertise, and dedication to empowering authors like me are commendable. You have taught me the intricacies of self-publishing and have also been instrumental in turning my manuscript into the book you now hold in your hands. Your support has made the dream of publishing *The Dawn of Hope* a tangible reality; I am deeply thankful for that.

A special thanks goes to my son Garth, whose talents have shaped the face of this project. Garth, your computer skills have been invaluable in bringing this book to life in the digital age. But your photography skills truly deserve a standing ovation—or perhaps a chuckle. Your valiant efforts to "make me look human" in the author's photo are heroic. Whether you succeeded is for the readers to decide. Still, your patience in capturing a father who's more comfortable behind a pulpit than in front of a camera is deeply appreciated. Your technical prowess and artistic eye have added professional polish to this work, and your ability to make me smile genuinely during our photo sessions has infused a bit of joy into every copy of this book. Thank you, son, for your skills and time and for making this journey a family affair. Many thanks, Bubba!

Finally, and most importantly, I extend my deepest gratitude to you, the readers of *The Dawn of Hope*. Whether you approach this book as a believer or seeker of truth, I am humbled and honored that you have chosen to spend your valuable time with these pages. Your willingness to engage with the ideas presented here, to read and meditate on the truths of God's Word, is the ultimate purpose of this book.

To those who already walk in faith, may this work deepen your understanding and strengthen your conviction. To those seeking, may you find the answers you seek and perhaps questions you hadn't thought to ask.

My heartfelt prayer for each of you is for growth—growth in grace, wisdom, and knowledge of our Lord and Savior, Jesus Christ. May the words within these pages not merely inform but transform, leading you into a richer, more full understanding of God's love and purpose for your life.

Thank you for joining me on this journey. May *The Dawn of Hope* be a light on your path, illuminating the way to deeper truth and abiding hope.

Scripture References Used
(CHRONOLOGICAL ORDER)

Chapter 10

Luke 2:21

Leviticus 12:3

Psalm 51:5

Galatians 5:3

Galatians 4:5

Deuteronomy 21:22–23

Galatians 3:13

Philippians 2:8

Matthew 1:21

Acts 13:23

Chapter 11

Luke 2:22–24

Leviticus 12:2–3

Leviticus 12:6

Luke 1:46–47

Romans 3:23

Chapter 12

Luke 2:25–27

Genesis 49:18

Isaiah 40:1

Luke 2:29–30

Chapter 13

Luke 2:28–32

2 Corinthians 6:2b

Chapter 14

Luke 2:33–35

Deuteronomy 30:19

Matthew 19:16–30

Mark 10:17–27

Luke 18:18–27

Luke 19:1–10

Chapter 15

Luke 2:36–37

John 12:43

Psalm 51:10

Chapter 16

Luke 2:38

Luke 1:68

Acts 4:10–12

Acts 1:11

Luke 2:25

Chapter 17

Luke 2:39

Matthew 1:19

Luke 3:23

Luke 2:52

Isaiah 9:6

Proverbs 22:6

Hebrews 4:15

Hebrews 10:25

Matthew 28:19a

Jeremiah 29:11

Chapter 18

Luke 2:40

John 1:14

Ephesians 2:8–9

Chapter 19

Luke 2:41–45

Psalm 27:8

Psalm 42:1

Chapter 20

Luke 2:46–51

Matthew 6:33

Matthew 7:7–8

Proverbs 2:1–5, v. 2

Chapter 21

Luke 2:52

John 1:1

Proverbs 8

Colossians 1:16

Colossians 2:3

James 3:15–17

Chapter 22

Luke 2:52

1 Timothy 4:8

Hebrews 4:15

3 John 1:2

1 Corinthians 6:19–20

Proverbs 3:7–8

1 Corinthians 9:27

Chapter 23

Luke 2:52

Hebrews 2:18

Matthew 3:17

Galatians 2:20

2 Peter 3:18

Matthew 25:23

Philippians 1:6

Chapter 24

Luke 2:52

John 2:23–25

John 6

Matthew 9:36

Mark 1:40–41

Mark 8:17–21

Luke 24:25–27

John 13:34

Luke 23:34

Matthew 18:21–22

John 11:35

Luke 10:21

Matthew 20:28

John 15:15

Luke 24:14–23

Matthew 23:13–36

Mark 2:1–12

Matthew 22:15–22

John 4:7–26
Philippians 2:5–8
Matthew 21:12–13
Matthew 9:36
Mark 1:40–41
Mark 2:17
1 Corinthians 10:31–33

Epilogue

Luke 2:19
Luke 2:51

Acknowledgements:

Philippians 1:3